Harry Martin

&

The Community Development Foundation

By Harry A. Martin
President Emeritus

*To Agnes Norris Martin, who stole my heart when we were in sixth grade.
She was born November 27, 1924, and she lived until March 11, 2015.
I received letters from her every day during my military service time.
Postage on those letters was a 3-cent stamp.
She made the best pound cakes ever.
I am thankful to God for the 67 years we had together.*

TABLE OF CONTENTS

Acknowledgements. 9

Preface 11

The Early Years. 13

Military Time. 17

The Summer of 1947 19

Following My Graduation in 1948. 25

An Area with Little Apparent Promise 29

Establishment of the North Mississippi District Forestry Office 31

Rural Depopulation-Urban Impaction. 39

Impact of Rural Development Work 43

Leadership and Influence of Congressman Whitten and Others. 45

Followship and Leadership. 47

The Brewer Community Leads the Way. 55

Some Traditional Problems: Liquor and Gambling. 57

A Demographic Profile of the Area. 59

Recognition of The Supporters of Good Government 61

    Good Government Representatives (Of Record) 62

    District I 62

    District II 62

    District III. 62

    District IV. 63

    District V. 63

    Executive Committee. 63

Changing the Structure of Leadership 69

The CDF Adopts A New Policy 71

CDF's Reaction to Change. 73

Rural Community Development Council and the CDF. 75

Expanding the Reach of CDF 77

Mr. Hoffman's Stop in Tupelo 79

The Importance of the Early Gasoline Service Stations. 83

The Lasting Influence of Mr. Hoffman's Visit 93

Additional Positive Influence of the CDF. 95

A World-Class Dairy Cattle Business 97

Development of The National Rural Development Act 103

Recruiting Mr. Krueger 105

Manufacturing Employment Sought for Area Workers. 107

Tradition 109

Tradition: A Roadblock to Progress 111

CDF's Industrialization Strategy. 113

The Contributions of Kyle and Erin Brown 119

The Influence of Leo Zuber 123

Beware the "Pet Project" Syndrome 125

Contributors to The Development of Northeast Mississippi. 127

The CDF's Influence on Growth and Development 133

    The Architects 134

    The Visionaries 135

Harry Martin and the Community Development Foundation | 7

    The Professionals 136

    Open-minded Volunteers. 137

"A Legacy of Excellence" Revisited 149

    Nick Chandler wrote on May 1, 2010. 149

    Tom Bailey wrote on September 1, 2010. 150

    On October 26, 2010, Gara Malesky wrote. 152

    Gara attached the following to her letter 153

Reflection. 155

Appendix I. 163

Appendix II 167

Appendix III. 175

Acknowledgements

I am grateful to Mrs. Carol Rupert and her husband, Daniel Rupert, of Tupelo, Mississippi, and Janet M. Martin for getting this very short report together; to the leaders of Oxford, Mississippi; to Mr. Neil W. White, III, Ms. Nancy Moore, Tannis Crabb, Sherry Kingsley, Renee' Dulaney, and many others including former CDF staff members and volunteers and leaders.

This book was sponsored by the Martin Family Trust. It is a personal report of some of my experiences and efforts. I am the only person remaining who saw the CDF's effort beginning in 1947 and lasting until August 21, 2000, when I retired from CDF as president emeritus and caregiver.

Harry A. Martin
August 2019

Preface: Birthday for CDF

The CDF of Tupelo and the Western North Carolina Development of Asheville, NC, were started by the nationally recognized Honorable True D. Morse. He required that for the first three years, he would be in charge of the director and would pay his salary and set the agenda for his work. Honorable Morse saw the changes that would come in the American South, where agriculture would see the largest loss of employees when and if automation was implemented.

Rural areas would need a different approach to progress or they would face economic decline. Both the CDF and the Western North Carolina Development of Asheville, NC, were successful and drew attention from national and international leaders. Morris McGough lead the NC group, and Sam Marshall was the first member he selected. I was asked to take over the Mississippi group from 1956-2000. Having been with Mr. Morse for all his early sessions in the interest of the Mississippi state leadership, I understood and practiced what he advocated. The notes in this report are some of my experiences.

The Early Years

Former President of the United States Dwight David Eisenhower once said, "We must be ready to dare all for our country. For history does not entrust the care of freedom to the weak or the timid." As one who has a lifetime membership in the American Legion as a result of my two-year tour in the Army Air Corps (which is now known as the United States Air Force) during World War II, I respect quotes such as this one found in American Legion publications. I am indeed thankful to God to have been born in America and to have served my country in her military.

I was born July 20, 1925, in Clarke County, Mississippi, which is east of Quitman. My mother, Bessie Rebecca Fleming Martin, and my father, Thomas Ed Martin, were both natives of Clarke County. My parents were the fourth generation of pioneer settlers from the 1700s of that area of Mississippi, and they were members of the second generation after the Civil War, for which members of both my mother's and my father's families served in the Confederate Army. Both of my parents came from large families of 12 children each. The period was one of economic difficulty, but because both families had good work ethics, they gave their children specific chores and work responsibilities at early ages to help support the family.

There were nine other children besides myself in my family who survived infancy and childhood; all were born between 1916 and 1931. One brother died from pneumonia when he was one year old. All my siblings and I were delivered at home by Dr. Watkins. Three of my sisters became nurses. They went to Hattiesburg, Mississippi, to earn their nursing credentials, and then they moved to New Orleans to work at Charity Hospital. I was 8 years old when Mother died from sepsis in 1933 at the age of 36. There were no antibiotics at that time to fight what was then called blood poisoning. Sepsis took the lives of many people during this era. We had no electricity or running water in our home until 1936, when the Tennessee Valley Authority made these modern conveniences available.

Both of my parents believed strongly in getting us at least through high school. The day after my mother's funeral, Daddy gathered us all together and said, "I do not plan to bring a woman into this house until all of you finish high school." Daddy married again in 1943 when most of us had gone to college or were married; he chose Miss Dora Avera, a lady who owned a dress pattern shop in Quitman, Mississippi, to be his wife. She was a wonderful woman whom we all loved.

I attended four public schools: Hebron Ridge, Cedar Creek, Hopewell, and Quitman High. Hopewell was where I met Agnes Norris, with whom I became friends in sixth grade and who later became my wife. Hopewell also was a school my great grandfather, who lost his left arm at the Battle of Petersburg, helped start after the Civil War, and it always maintained high academic standards.

Social life on the farm as we grew up was limited to the Baptists, the Methodists, and to family gatherings at our grandparents' houses. Agnes Norris, my sweetheart, was a member of the Antioch Baptist Church; she was baptized in Okatuppa Creek, which is on the Mississippi/Alabama state line, on Mississippi Highway 18 about 18 miles east of Quitman. I attended Elim Baptist Church about four miles from the Antioch Church on Highway 18 east of Quitman. I was baptized in water from the Rocky Creek because, in those days, country churches did not have baptistries. We had a Model T Ford that we drove to church. Because the country was in the Depression, there was not much money with which to purchase gas. The car was driven very little, but we always drove it to church.

Baptizing was a big event which usually happened on Sunday afternoon. Because there was no physical facility, after the morning service, the boys went one direction, and the girls went another into the woods to change their clothes from wet to dry. Usually, several candidates for baptism participated in each ceremony over which the minister presided; baptisms happened in the summer months while the weather was warm. Both Agnes's church and mine were built by our grandparents, who settled in the area in the 1830s-1850s.

Agnes and I both attended Hopewell School and graduated.

Quitman High School, under the leadership of Professor Zack Huggins, had the reputation of producing only the best leaders in the state. Hopewell also had an exemplary record of excellence, which was an opportunity that was good for Agnes and me; we remained friends and motivated each other to move on and make meaningful contributions in life.

Agnes and I both became members of the 4-H Club at Hopewell, and we were both also members of the BYPU (Baptist Young People Union). When we transferred from Hopewell Junior High to Quitman High School, we continued our 4-H projects that we had begun earlier in our lives. In the summer during high school, Agnes and I, along with several hundred other state-wide representatives, had the opportunity to attend Mississippi State University. We all attended numerous events and project training, and we were selected for inclusion in trips to the Gulf Coast. Outside of our families and friends, church, and school, the cooperative extension service that administered the 4-H Club activities had a major positive impact on our lives. The Extension staff was very helpful in getting us involved in quality educational activities. It is because the Clarke County Extension staff and the superintendent greatly influenced the direction our lives took that we recently, in 2018, created a scholarship position in Lee and Clarke Extensions to give others the help that Agnes and I got at Mississippi State. We were granted a vision beyond the local limits of our lives that there could be opportunities beyond those offered locally. The gift of the Extension 4-H was fulfilled; it was one of the ways Agnes and I thought we could repay some of the help and special attention we had received to help us succeed in choosing the direction we would take in later years.

I also became very active in the Future Farmers of America (FFA) and participated in school debates, public debates, and parliamentary procedure contests. Those activities enabled Agnes and me to go to Mississippi State for additional state events in which hundreds of youth participated each year.

In 1942, I finished high school at the age of 16; on Senior Class Night, I was given a baby pacifier for being the "Baby of the Class." By the time I was 14, I had bought and paid for 40 acres of land; when I graduated from high school, I had accumulated 36 head of cattle and hogs. The next week after graduation from high school, I bought a $4 ticket and boarded the GM&O Rebel at the Quitman depot with a 4-H Club scholarship to enter the School of Agriculture at Mississippi State.

During this time, the College of Agriculture under the Director of Programs Dean E.B. Colmer advertised that he had a job opening. Since I was living on a limited budget, I applied for the job that paid $0.20 an hour and that began at 4 a.m. five days a week. I was hired and found myself working in the field of a tree farm composed of multiple plots of experimental work on crops and livestock and recording each assignment on the farm. The professor who was the leader of this job and I got along, and I applied again for the job a second year. The position required whoever was hired to keep records for all the professors in the School of Agriculture, assist with the copier, and maintain absolute secrecy of the exams and their contents from the students. I was hired again, and because I did well with this assignment, I became a trustworthy employee of the dean, who later became Mississippi State President Clay Lyle. It occurs to me later in my life that the goodwill of these leaders and their friends helped me tremendously and directed my service in Tupelo, Mississippi.

Military Time

Having completed two years of work on my degree by my 18th birthday in 1943, I boarded a bus from Mississippi State to the Columbus Air Force Base in Lowndes County, Mississippi, and enlisted in the Air Corps for cadet training because the United States was heavily involved in fighting in World War II. I was accepted and sent to Camp Shelby, Mississippi, to be sworn into military service. From there, I traveled to Miami Beach, Florida, for basic training, orientation, and testing. Because I was among the one in five who passed, I went to Lockbourne Air Force Base in Columbus, Ohio, where B-17 bombers were repaired, and pilots were trained before entering active war service, for air cadet orientation and on-line experience. The first eight months I served in the Air Corps were spent in cadet training, which culminated in a cadet becoming a pilot, a bombardier, or a navigator, which I was. Navigation required exceptional skills in mathematics to calculate the exact location of the target; we did not have radar technology at this time. We were required to become proficient and accurate in three methods: radio, dead recognition (visual), and celestial. Navigation, which was my training field, required calculating the heading needed to reach the destination. It seems simple, but one had to deal with wind direction, the speed of the plane, daylight/darkness, terrain, whether the plane was over land or water, and numerous other variables.

I was then sent to the University of Pittsburgh for classes in physics, meteorology, and mathematics. I learned about the locations and names of stars, clouds, and weather; if weather happened to be an interference factor, the navigator in the plane had to tell the pilot to adjust the flight pattern, and the navigator had to plot a new course if the pilot issued that directive.

While there, I made the cadet basketball team, and we played against several other military units in the region.

It was there I learned that Mississippi had the poorest standard of living in all of the United States and that our state had a very slow growth rate in economics compared to all the other states; I learned everything except what was wrong with our culture to cause this negative status. Because of these discoveries, I determined to collect and learn as much about economic growth and development as possible. Even though I did not enroll in classes, I began gathering books and information as these materials became available to me.

After graduating as a navigator from air cadet training in 1945, I had a choice of signing up for three years in the Air Force Reserves and being commissioned as an officer or going home the next day because President Harry Truman had declared that the war was over. I chose to catch a ride home the next day; I returned to Quitman and later re-enrolled at Mississippi State.

During my last two years at Mississippi State, Dr. Lyle recommended me to Dr. Colmer for a position that required me to work in his office to keep the records on the farm and to mimeograph all the professors' students' examinations. It was with the encouragement of Dean Colmer that I came to Tupelo, Mississippi, on a special project at the end of my junior year. Meanwhile, Dr. Clay Lyle was making advancements in Mississippi State College leadership and would later become President of Mississippi State University.

The Summer of 1947

I was asked by Dean E.B. Colmer of Mississippi State College (now University) to spend six weeks during the summer break of 1947 to look at and write a report about the new idea of community development in Tupelo, Mississippi. I was to write about Mr. True D. Morse's efforts to make the transition of the first major change in technology done in America of moving the agricultural economy from human and animal farming to mostly machines and technology. Lee County was not listed as one of the top ten industrial employee centers prior to CDF's being chartered in 1948; however, in the middle 1960s, it became a county that had more per-capita income from off-the-farm income (an income stream generated from work off the farm) than above-farm income (income solely generated by the farm). This development allowed Lee County to become more independent on more than 5,200 families' incomes instead of depending upon mainly cotton and the milking of cows as the major income. The cotton fields and the dairy farms were very positive things for workers who left the farm but kept their residences on the farm. They usually had much stronger work ethics and vocations than the regular workers. These were good qualities in workers that new industries found appealing. Few people knew that this change at the time would effectively change the status of the local rural communities. Mr. True D. Morse proposed to develop a plan for Mr. George McLean, publisher of the *Tupelo Daily Journal*, the local newspaper. Mr. Morse was the head of the Doane Agricultural Service in St. Louis, Missouri. He was a most respected visionary and planner in the field of rural development in the United States.

Mr. M.M. Winkler, a certified public accountant in Tupelo, operated a regional CPA firm during this time and had worked with Mr. Morse on very successful projects in other areas of the South and had become personally acquainted with him and his firm and the success that was achieved. Mr. Winkler arranged for Mr. Morse and Mr. McLean to confer in Tupelo, and as a result, Mr. McLean and the *Daily Journal* entered a three-year program for $6,000 to develop what became known as the "Tupelo Plan," which was a radical movement away from the accepted provincial approach to solving economic problems. Mr. Morse's plan mandated that leaders of at least three counties had to be included. After many sessions and modifications of the original structure, the original program succeeded.

Mr. McLean had many wonderful personal characteristics, including listening to other people who had new ideas, giving thought to its relationship to the area, and looking for people who would deliver results. Early on, I learned how to serve with him and understand that he was motivated by pushing projects forward, which he did, as he underwrote the new "Tupelo Plan" project proposed by Mr. Morse. Rather than seek financial help from others, a decision was made for the *Daily Journal* to finance the project. Even though Mr. Morse became easily irritated, there was a special characteristic he possessed, and that was how excited he became as CDF gained achievement and recognition for positive economic change.

When I came to the Community Development Foundation in 1956, there were 60 organized Rural Community Development Councils (RCDC) in five counties. In 1956, CDF expanded from the original three counties. Because of the effort of the RCDC program in the 60 rural communities and the CDF, this area was becoming an example of successfully retaining the rural population in the community when more jobs and better pay were available. The details of this effort by the community leaders are demonstrated in the public support for Harry A. Martin and the Community Development Foundation.

This era proved, in Northeast Mississippi, that economic development does not follow political lines, and when community and elected leaders work together in a coordinated effort, positive things happen in growth. It was common in those years to state that Tupelo was the "city without city limits." As a result of Mr. Morse's plan for regionalization, the Northeast

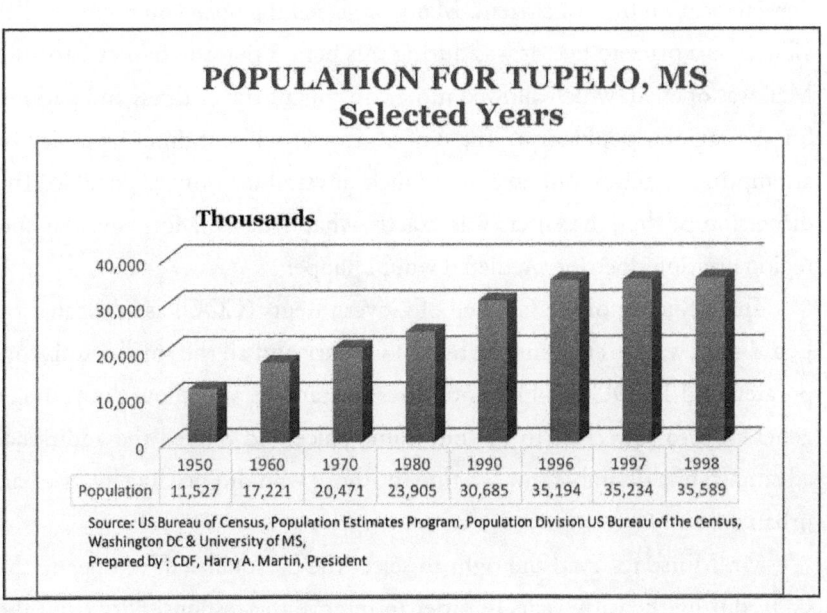

area of Mississippi became nationally recognized for the stabilization of its population in rural areas, above most others. As most people know, the attitude in the city has changed and is returning, in the opinion of some, to more provincial thinking.

Even though the number of jobs was growing, and annexed areas closed more home sales, the city of Tupelo's population started to slow in the 1990s. The three most common reasons given were schools, taxes, and law enforcement. The dispersion of the job centers allowed more choice of residential location by area citizens. Many preferred the open county or smaller villages as a place to live. It was during this period that the Barnes Crossing Mall was opened, which allowed more convenient travel access and parking for the region's population. The city of Tupelo will continue its policy of attempting to annex and take in as much physical territory as possible. The dispersion of the job centers was exactly what True D. Morse's vision and regionalization doctrine predicted would happen.

The influence of the Council of Governments (COG) as advocated by Leo Zuber, was an enabling act by Lee County and all the smaller unincorporated and RCDC rural communities to stabilize and allow the younger generation to stay close to the old home place and offered the additional advantage of a desirable rural setting for those who did not like living in an urban area.

Mr. Morse reserved the right to select the personal staff to operate the CDF during the early years in order to remove the responsibility from the local people who had yet to perceive what change would be necessary for the region to advance. He recognized the three political factions present and wanted to be sure that qualified professionals were selected independently from local politics.

Mr. and Mrs. Harry Martin, 1948

Following My Graduation in 1948

I graduated in 1948 with a degree in agricultural administration. I returned to Quitman that same year and married my childhood sweetheart, Agnes Norris. We settled down to live happily in my hometown.

I mentioned earlier Dean Colmer, who gave me a choice of going to Hattiesburg, Brookhaven, or Tupelo, and I chose Tupelo. He asked me to do a special project for him when I was a junior in the summer of 1947. That project involved spending six weeks of summer break examining and writing a report about the new idea of community development in Tupelo. Mr. True D. Morse, who was the head of the Doane Agricultural Service in St. Louis, Missouri, proposed to develop a plan for Mr. George McLean, who was the publisher of the *Daily Journal*, the local newspaper in Tupelo. Mr. Morse was a highly respected visionary and planner in the field of rural development in the United States. Later, during the Eisenhower Administration, he was appointed undersecretary of agriculture.

My first mission in Tupelo was to find out how True D. Morse got to Tupelo and to meet with Mr. George McLean. I found out that a company that offered accounting services had customers in St. Louis, Missouri, and Mr. Winkler was doing work for his firm. Mr. Winkler was always looking for ways to improve the economic standards of the region. Recorded history overlooks key figures involved in the growth of the area; when I came here in 1947, I learned that there were many folks involved, but they were not devoted and organized enough to do much about creating change.

In early September 1948, the district Extension agent asked me if I would be interested in being the assistant county agent in charge of the

Boys 4-H Club. The Lee County Extension Service was led by W.J. "Red" Pernell, who was a tall red-haired gentleman, seasoned in Extension work and respected in our state and in the region. In the early 1950s, his staff received National Superior Service Recognition for its pioneering of early rural community development work. Mr. Pernell, Mr. Pat Dougherty, and Mr. George McLean were all visionaries. Mr. Pernell was the organizational, tactical contact, and clearance agent; Mr. Dougherty was the glue that held the rural people and the townspeople together during the formative years of the idea of community development in Tupelo.

Dean Colmer, Mr. Ed Stanley, who was the district Extension agent, and Mr. Pernell, who was the county agent, were involved with the development of the Tupelo Plan by Mr. Morse, Mr. Pat Dougherty, and Mr. George McLean. The Mississippi State School of Agriculture, the cooperative extension service, and Home Demonstration Agents – in addition to Mr. Dougherty's contacts in 13 counties – helped with the financing and refinancing of hundreds of farm projects and mortgages in the Tupelo/Lee County area. Many groups came to observe the Agricultural Agency Council, which was comprised of the extension service, the Production Credit Association, the Federal Land Bank, the Farmers Home Administration, the Farm Bureau, the Soil Conservation Service, and other agencies. The involvement of the extension service at the county, district, state, and national levels and the leadership of other federal agencies have not been adequately recognized. The professionals in the county and Home Demonstration offices in Lee, Itawamba, Monroe, Prentiss, Pontotoc, and Chickasaw counties – along with the State Department of Vocational Education and the high schools of the area – all furnished the professional leadership for the early (RCDC) organizations.

Other groups that furnished subsidy and support were the civic clubs in all the counties. Since there were multiple counties involved, often included were regional leaders and decision-makers who had to be supportive of the effort to promote community farm and home development and coordinate economic growth in an area with very low per-capita income. The economy of the region before the World War II years was a rural agricultural enterprise. Production and processing based on this cooperative effort were essential to the success of the Community Development Foundation; additionally, these elements have not been given full credit for their contribution to our success. Mr. Morse, who was the nationally recognized foremost agricultural consultant, was also highly competent in accounting, management, and financial evaluation. The mid-section of our area, including the hills and the delta, caught the attention of all the agencies. Along with Mr. Dougherty's and Mr. Pernell's influences in the early days, plus dozens of other farm specialists, such as Mr. Paul McElroy of the Federal Compress, representatives of the Carnation Milk Company, Mr. Ray Purnell, and Mr. Charlie Brooks, father of Tommy Brooks, leaders visited 5,200 farmers in Lee County alone to promote dairy farming.

Mr. Gale Carr, a native of Missouri, was an outstanding dairyman and was the person who established the Tupelo area Artificial Insemination Association; he and Mr. W.L. Wood from Arkansas formed Carr-Meyers Dairy. The Artificial Insemination Association was the first in Mississippi; its advanced technology was ahead of that at Mississippi State, and it reached 15,000 cows annually. Mr. Cecil Trawick was the managing technician. Mr. Morse recommended that the Chamber, the TAAIA, which was the agricultural marketing association, and the Lee County Jersey Cattle Club all be absorbed by the Community Development Foundation (CDF) in 1948.

The involvement and empowerment of the area beyond the county approach that Mr. Morse insisted on proved to be essential to the early development stage. These public agents of the state and local government agencies provided a commitment to be competitive and innovative in how the agency they represented could provide projects to assist in the future growth and development of the economy. Projects included the formation of the Tombigbee Valley Water Management District Organizations, led by Olen Pound of Pontotoc, Mississippi, and Mr. Dougherty and the Town Creek Master Water Shed Flood Control District, led by the Soil Conservation Service and Mr. Beasley. Thirty-six flood control structures that protected Tupelo and the West Fork of the Tombigbee, known as the Town

Creek, from flooding were built. Support came from Mr. Roy C. Adams, the Northern District highway commissioner, after much encouragement from the 56 Northern District RCDC communities. This support helped in many ways, but it primarily helped the rural areas of Northeast Mississippi in getting built the best secondary highway system in the state, which provided the means for many rural citizens to move about and to move their farm products into commerce and travel to off-farm jobs growing in business and industry.

An Area with Little Apparent Promise

These were very hard times in the economic history of Northeast Mississippi. Leaders have been reluctant to point out that the educational level of Northeast Mississippi is generally lower than that of other sections of the state. A key factor to economic growth is per-capita income. Northeast Mississippi leaders did not speak of the deficiencies, but the population was aware of them. It was the post-World War II period with hundreds of veterans looking for jobs to provide for the future of their families. The prevailing work culture was milking cows and growing cotton, with some employment in labor-intensive enterprises, such as agricultural processing jobs at Carnation Milk. At this time, Northeast Mississippi was a typical Southern rural area with little promise for economic growth and a comparatively low literacy count. To get ahead in the economic growth effort, something had to be done better and in a more aggressive way.

Establishment of the North Mississippi District Forestry Office

The Appalachian Region Commission Road, and CDF's Council of Government

In the 1950s, Mr. Adams also headed a committee at CDF to promote the establishment of the North Mississippi District Forestry Office. This action helped to bring forestry to the forefront as another source of income from idle and non-income producing land.

Assisting Mr. Adams was Mr. Grady Smith, a local businessman, who was the major political point person for Mississippi's Governor J.P. Coleman. Under Mr. Adams' leadership, Community Development Foundation supported the "Peter Pine Planting Programs," which promoted the planting of 16 million pine seedlings that would later be one of the selling points to qualify the area to document and recruit the Norbord plant, which is an international leader in forest product processing and marketing, at Guntown.

In addition to Mr. Grady Smith, the local Western Auto Store owner, other outstanding leaders such as Mr. Kirby Faucette, the Gulf Oil distributor; Mr. Reese Senter, a concrete maker; and Junior Hancock, restaurant owner, were key players in getting the state and federal government to fund the construction of the Appalachian Regional Commission Road in Tupelo. This industrial access road opened traffic to the major job centers in Northwest Mississippi, including the rapidly growing medical center. The CDF, upon the request of Congressman Jamie Whitten and Commissioner Hershel Jumper of the State Highway Department, helped with developing the ARC corridor from Batesville to Tupelo, Highway 78 from Memphis, Tennessee, to Birmingham, Alabama, and the highway from Fulton, Mississippi, to Huntsville, Alabama.

The CDF assisted with these projects. The CDF's Council of Governments (C.O.G.) staff, led by Ms. Georgia Webb, had two graduate planners, Mr. Nick Chandler, and Mr. Woody Sample, who provided excellent project preparation and documentation. The Appalachian Regional Commission (ARC) corridor was to be the third major auto or motorized vehicle highway put into place, which would make Tupelo and Lee County the most accessible point in Northeast Mississippi; this access would allow the city to serve as a major regional center as Mr. Morse predicted it could become in his 1947 plan.

The two major railroad crossings built in the late 1800s (1872 and 1885) are responsible for Tupelo becoming the central city, even though Verona, Saltillo, and Plantersville had been early agricultural service towns before Tupelo was formed. The first federally funded road was built in the 1912-1925 period. Porter Carothers, Lee County's Representative in the state Legislature from 1844-1923, established and authorized for the first time a state agency to work with federal highway programs. That agency is now the Mississippi Highway Commission. It is and has been the source of much help in developing the economy and accessibility to Northeast Mississippi. Mr. Carothers, who was involved in many important events, worked cooperatively with his friend, Senator Bankhead of Alabama. Their friendship had developed during their service in the Army of the Confederacy. Senator Bankhead helped to secure support for one of the first, if not the first, coast to coast good roads as the roads were called at that time. This one was named the Bankhead in honor of Senator John Bankhead; it was a gravel road that ran from Birmingham to Sulligent, Alabama. The Bankhead Highway eventually came to Tupelo and passed along Main Street to what is now Clayton Avenue, where Mr. Carothers lived. It became US 78 and 278 after the old Bankhead Highway; both brought two major highways in the early 1900s to Tupelo.

Additionally, Mr. Porter Carothers was involved in public policies, including getting public schools formed in Lee County. The highway continued to Belden, which was known as West Tupelo, as the old Belden Road through New Albany on the main street that is still known as Bankhead Street, all the way to the West Coast. Belledeer Street joins the Bankhead Highway, and it was built on the line where Itawamba and Pontotoc counties once joined.

The oldest house in the area was built in 1880 for Mr. and Mrs. Porter and Elizabeth Carothers. Across the street was a house built for the Honorable Pete and Mrs. Mitchell. He was wounded in World War II, and he was a very popular servant of the public courts. The Mitchell and Savery homes, as well as the Carothers home, sat on land that was once in Itawamba County before the formation of Lee County in 1876. Belledeer Street was at the point on the street of the Carothers house and the Mitchell home; it was the division line between Pontotoc and Itawamba counties, which later changed counties. The Carothers house had four acres; it was a typical "dog trot" house, and it was occupied later by Mr. and Mrs. Huey Long. Agnes and I purchased the home from Mrs. Long in 1972, and we have lived there for 47 years. Other celebrities who lived in the area were the Lt. Governor Honorable Sam Lumpkin, whose home sold recently, and Mrs. Rex Reed, who moved there after selling their home and dairy farm to the city of Tupelo to create Ballard Park.

Mr. and Mrs. Grimes (she was Elvis Presley's schoolteacher) built a home on the corner of Clayton and Belledeer; they soon built another on Elvis Presley Boulevard near Elvis's home and the homes of Mr. and Mrs. J.C. Whitehead and many other Bancorp leaders. Elvis visited the Savery home on his visit back to Tupelo and East Tupelo, his hometown.

Belledeer Street joins the Bankhead Highway; it was built as one of the first detours on the line where Itawamba and Pontotoc counties once joined. According to the state agency in charge, the Carothers home is eligible for historic recognition should its owner choose to pursue it.

The significance of this era is the important changes in the economic growth, driving change that took place in moving the economic future toward where Mr. True D. Morse had hoped the leadership would move to a regional approach; he insisted that a multi-county effort be implemented, and the Community Development Foundation was chartered to operate in a 50-mile territory. It involved leaders from this area to project its influence. With my 44.5 years with the CDF as a paid manager, I also had given eight years as an assistant on the staff of county agent Mr. Red Pernell. As an associate county agent, I became well acquainted with the importance and the value of building good relations among the large rural population and learning how they could be motivated to act on important issues. We learned from having civic club members visit the rural people in meetings, and this program received national recognition for its successful work.

There is a good collection of historical information on the Bankhead family at the public library in Sulligent, Alabama. Upon a visit there, I was advised that the Bankhead homeplace was in the area and that his house was still standing. I took a "windshield tour" of the house and discovered that it has many of the same characteristics as the Carothers' house in which we presently reside. Both houses were built on acreages just outside of their nearby towns one outside of Sulligent, Alabama, and the other outside of Tupelo, Mississippi.

Upon reading the information sent by Sarah Chittom and the state historical group, and from copies of the *Mississippi House Journal*, I learned that Representative Carothers not only introduced legislation but also was successful in getting it passed with emphasis on developing statewide inter-county highways, which authorized the establishment of the State Highway Department, including the appointment of a highway commissioner, and this led to the state's longtime reputation of having one of the best highway systems in the nation. This recognition has been and continues to be a very important part of the growth and development of one of the nation's most rural states. My observation of this action by Mr. Carothers was exactly what Mr. True D. Morse, when he formed the CDF, said had to be done if we were to grow an economy and compete in a national and international economy. Representative Carothers might have been Lee County's first and one of our best pioneer regional developers. The information in the *Mississippi House Journal* also pointed out that another very strong commitment Representative Carothers had was to cover Lee County with schools that were conveniently located to the population with authority for local parents to guide and support the neighborhood schools.

I discovered this strength in rural development when I came to work here in 1948. My assignment was to lead the Boys' 4-H Clubs, which held monthly meetings at the school buildings during school hours. It was with my associate, Mrs. Margaret Nichols, who was the Girls' 4-H Club leader, that we visited twenty-four public schools that were all well-supported and all with strong administrations and discipline and extremely dedicated teachers.

The neighborhoods around these rural schools and the buildings became the center of the organization and promotion of the Rural Community Development Councils (RCDC) program initiated by the "Tupelo Plan," as developed by Mr. Morse and that was started by Mr. Sam Marshall and Mr. W.J. "Red" Pernell. The success of the RCDC program was greatly enhanced by the leadership of the schools, the Cooperative Extension agents, and the leadership of the Boys' and Girls' 4-H Clubs and Home Demonstration Clubs of each community. The schools defined the community center for those of us involved in the administration of the program. *The Journal of the House of Representatives of the State of Mississippi* recorded the long and tiring effort of Representative Carothers to get these schools approved by the Legislature in the 1904-1916 period.

My father was the grandson of John Henry Martin, II, a Confederate veteran who lost his left arm at the Battle of Petersburg. After the war, my grandfather led the formation of a rural settlement in Clarke County, and he was the chairman of the Board of Trustees that formed the Hopewell

Public School that my father attended and where I attended. Obviously, the veterans of the Civil War came home determined to help their children get a good education. That era produced quality educated citizens who were able to compete admirably in their communities. I did not realize how important good academic schools were until I enrolled at Mississippi State University. It was at this point I saw my classmates who did not attend a quality school have much difficulty competing in the university classroom. As I reflect on my career, I fully appreciate those early leaders who provided the opportunities for my generation and me.

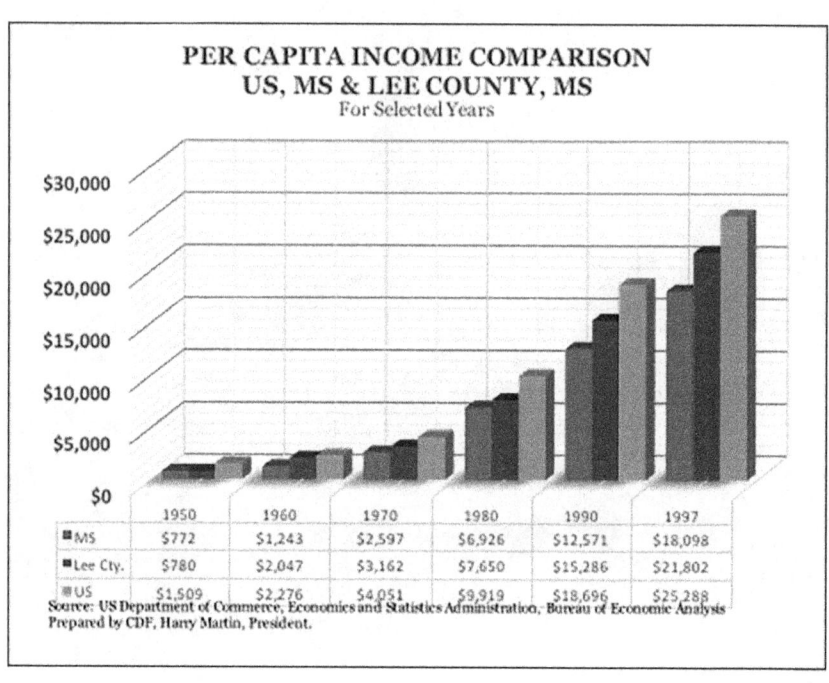

Rural Depopulation-Urban Impaction

The economic numbers and growth for the area were improving, but during the 1950s, many families were selling their small farms and moving to the industrial cities of the North and Midwest. Population figures show that almost 20,000 people – the population equivalent of Pontotoc County during this time – left the Tupelo trade area during this period. This period of history was when technological advancement in agriculture in the United States of America created a situation that became the largest social, economic, and political change in the history of the country. This period was known as the "Rural Depopulation-Urban Impaction" movement. Nationwide, people left their birthplaces and went into large cities looking for employment. There simply was not enough farm income to support returning veterans and their families.

Along with this migration, the elimination of the many conservative family values of the South occurred. In the past, as many as three generations lived in the same household. Moral and social values had been closely guarded by all, including grandparents. Rural Depopulation-Urban Impaction would change the cultural, educational, economic, social, moral, and family values that we all knew at that time.

Agriculture was the first industry to bring to us advances in major technology such as 2-, 4-, 8- and 12-row tractors and cultivators, herbicide to control weeds and grass, combines and mechanical harvesters of crops. This technology released thousands of people in rural areas from jobs on farms across America. This major turning point in the counties' cultural and economic life was recognized by a few leaders in rural America, one of whom was Mr. True D. Morse, developer of the "Tupelo Plan." In addition to Tupelo, he also presented his plan in Asheville, North Carolina, and it spread fast to several other areas of the South. An organization known as the Southeastern Community Development Association (SECDA) formed in 1952 in Cherokee, North Carolina. The CDF was a charter member. Organizations in North Carolina, Georgia, Tennessee, Mississippi, Kentucky, and West Virginia were the primary promoters of this movement. Thus, the scene was set for the seeming happenstance of Mr. Hoffman's significant visit to help change the direction of Northeast Mississippi's economic future. (Refer to Mr. Hoffman's Stop in Tupelo on page 83.)

One characteristic of rural areas was the conservatism of lenders, who, in many instances, resisted change and progressive ideas in the areas of industrial and economic growth. The small group of SECDA leaders, who utilized the influence of Mr. Morse, worked to form the basic recommendations for the National Rural Development programs. These programs strengthened the support for the rural water systems that allowed farm and expanded rural housing to exist.

The programs' increased support improved roads and made housing loans available through such agencies as the Farmers Home Administration, the Veterans Administration, and others. The programs also strengthened support for rural small businesses and farming by producing technical training and advisory resources. This program helped stabilize the migration from the farms into the urban areas. At that time, more people in the country lived on farms, but today, because of migration into urban areas, more people live in cities. One result has been a breakdown of traditional conservative morals and family values.

As a result of serving on the national commission, our groups recommended project strategies for the National Rural Development program. National attention was given to what was going on in Tupelo, Mississippi, and Asheville, North Carolina, and other rural places in the nation. Mr. Morris McGough and I received numerous invitations to speak and to do workshops nationwide. One was arranged by the secretary of agriculture and coordinated by the USDA Graduate School in Silver Springs, Maryland.

Following this presentation, the graduate school arranged for me to travel to speak to seven regional rural development workshops in all areas within the 48 continental states; additionally, a national program committee invited me to do a presentation at its conferences sponsored by the Economic Development Administration (EDA) at Wingspread in Racine, Wisconsin. The National Rural Development Conference, in cooperation with EDA, limited attendance to 45 people. Included were high-level government specialists, university experts, and operators of economic development organizations. I presented a speech on "Industrial Development Needs at the Local Level." The three-day conference emphasized the economy of rural America and the state of our knowledge of rural America and the state of our knowledge on rural development policies and programs. Mr. Morse was the first national leader to promote industrialization of the rural areas.

Impact of Rural Development Work

Representative Carothers was not present to witness the success of the rural development work of Northeast Mississippi during the 1947-2000 era, but what he did made it much easier to accomplish than it would have been otherwise. This feat should be a reminder to all of us not to give credit to single individuals for what has been done, but to be appreciative of the situation in our community that others gave us to work with; I have always considered it my job to make whatever improvement I could and pass it along for others to contribute as they are able to do so.

Little credit has been given locally to many significant and outstanding events and people who have helped make Tupelo and the surrounding counties the center of Northeast Mississippi. The second motorized road of significant importance to be built for automobiles was the Natchez Trace Parkway roadway, which was completed in 2000. The third instance of significant impact, much yet to be realized, was the designation of Mississippi Highway 6 and US 78 as a part of corridor X and Z as part of the Appalachian Regional Commission Regional Economic Development Plan as done by Representative Jamie Whitten and supported by Governor John Bell Williams and a committee from the CDF. Mr. Whitten asked the CDF planning staff to lay out the Batesville, Mississippi, to Huntsville, Alabama, route location. Representative Jamie Whitten had previously ordered that the new highway had to come through Tupelo after two earlier efforts to pass the new four-lane program had failed.

The 1987 four-lane Mississippi Highway Program was headed by Mr. Morris Lewis of Indianola, Mississippi; because of Mr. Lewis's bad health,

Mr. Mark Ledbetter with WTVA of Tupelo assumed the impetus for the highway project. He was the CDF chairman, and he and other Tupelo citizens added to the strength of these other mentioned projects. Additional support came from Highway Commissioner Zach Stewart, who deserves much credit for the North Mississippi expanded involvement in four-lane highway construction. Credit must also be given to the cooperation Mr. Stewart received from the Central District Commissioner who provided the two votes needed from the three-man State Highway Commission to give the Northern District more miles of four-lane highways than the other two districts. The Memphis, Tupelo, and Birmingham interstate designation is important; however, the Huntsville and Birmingham and X and Z both come through Tupelo. In the future, when the International Highway 69 to Canada and Mexico and South America is complete to the Batesville I-69, the connection will add significant possible benefits to Tupelo's future and will become another major economic development project.

As I have written before, even though the number of jobs was rising and annexed areas closed more home sales, the city of Tupelo's population started to slow in the 1990s. The three most common reasons given were schools, taxes, and law enforcement. The dispersion of the job centers allowed more choice of residential location by area citizens. Many preferred the open county or smaller villages in which to live.

Leadership and Influence of Congressman Whitten and Others

As I reflect on my career, I am reminded of the occasion when Jamie and Rebecca Thompson Whitten (from Saltillo) had asked me to be the purchasing agent for them to refurbish their Charleston, Mississippi, home with specific antiques. After Jamie Whitten found the furniture that Mrs. Whitten wanted, I sent a bob-type truck over to their home so they could come from Washington, D.C., after the next election to retire. Mr. and Mrs. Whitten were more than ready to seek the privilege of retiring and coming back to Mississippi to enjoy the rest of their lives in Charleston.

Many of the major federal projects, such as the Tombigbee Waterway, were underway but not finished. The Town Creek master plan was drawn up to provide a way to control floods on our best agricultural lands and in industrial, residential, and commercial areas of towns such as Tupelo. This plan required several years of Congressman Whitten's leadership in Washington, D.C. While working with Mrs. Whitten, I asked if it would be acceptable if a small delegation from Tupelo came over one day while they were at home during sessions of Congress; she agreed provided she and Jamie could be a part of the decision-making about who would be invited. They agreed to invite three couples to spend the day at their home after it was furnished. The three were J.C. and Mary Whitehead; Harry and Ruth Rutherford; my wife, Agnes, and me. After meeting and talking with the Whittens, this group became more aware of the Whittens' greatest concerns and what it would take to keep them in Washington, D.C. The primary concern was that the district leadership would need to give the congressman more relief in running his election campaign and to help relieve him and his wife of the major physical effort they usually had to expend and to be sure the financial support was in place. Buddy Bishop, Mr. Whitten's chief of staff, was present. We committed to him and promised that we would help achieve the Whittens' request.

J.C. Whitehead worked with the bankers and others to look after the financial aspect of the re-election campaign; Harry Rutherford worked with Bill Miles of Fulton to coordinate the information and media aspect, and I worked with Buddy Bishop on scheduling and campaign organization. Representative Whitten probably deserved as much credit as any other individual in the economic and physical development of Northeast Mississippi.

Followship and Leadership

There is an old saying that when there is no "followship," there is no "leadership"; and when there is no "learning," there is no "teaching." One of the great characteristics of Lee County is that its strength comes from the strong conservative spiritual values held by many well-informed rural and town citizen families. Where there is a consensus, things begin to happen. I have witnessed this occurrence many times in my work. I have seen the clean sweep of the courthouse in 1947, the removal of the Phoenix City criminal element, and the replacement of low efficient judicial people, the support of the Franklin Graham Crusade in the 1990s, and the strong support of the better jobs and additional job programs of the CDF for the past 60 years.

Early in the 1950s, there was a movement to hard-surface rural roads so that every church in the county could be reached via a paved road. The supervisors chose to issue bonds to pave the roads, and this paving later became a major factor in the understanding of the area because paved roads meant that workers could get to their jobs and back home without being handicapped by impassable roads. I saw the leadership work together and plant sixteen million pine seedlings in the 1950s; those trees led to erosion control and to more forestry income. Furthermore, the planting led to major processing for Northeast Mississippi and boosting of employment.

It is possible that those of us involved in growing and developing a large community failed to recognize the strength and diversity of the leadership in the total community. Perhaps a large part of the leadership team was not engaged in the broad and complex segments that influence growth factors, which may have resulted in spotted success while leaving behind big geographic areas that were not moving with the entire body of community action. It appears to me that there is a perception that only certain individuals, mostly in the central population zone, influenced change. As a result of this perception, many of the natural and qualified leaders in the larger community assumed that their leadership was not important; consequently, they occupied themselves with "pet projects" that may not have contributed to the growth and development of the larger community.

If one examines the philosophy of Mr. Morse's original plan, known as the Tupelo Plan, it becomes evident that he insisted that there had to be multiple and diverse geographic units activated in the larger (multi-county) area. Each unit was encouraged to adopt two local goals annually – plus one goal that the larger council chose – to ensure that all had a major impact or concentration and a connection with each other, sharing and receiving each other's successes and failures. This plan allowed hundreds of people to become involved and to participate in the process of focused growth and development and to experience the satisfaction of having been a part of the growth and development of the community and the rewards therein. The successful plans perceived that a detailed, active, and productive organizational structure had to be in place.

The organization was the Community Development Foundation (CDF), and its loyal affiliated groups were to be not only the vehicle that growth and development rode on, but also the one that allowed its participants and hundreds of affiliated local organizations a stage or platform on which to perform and show their successful projects and accomplishments. After the CDF was formed, I successfully helped the group to perform this role. After 1948, the CDF referred to the area within a fifty-mile radius of Tupelo, rather than an organization that most people associated with only Tupelo and Lee County. My experience with maintaining the balance and involvement of volunteer community projects, plus keeping them motivated to complete and bring results, was often side-tracked or derailed in many other places because of a "pet project" of some eager individual.

Obviously, I was not influenced by the patrons of some of these pet projects. They injected themselves into the community development process because the "pet project pushers" saw how they could get their pet projects done by others. Many of them had been personally involved with the two executives who had preceded me at CDF. They had all experienced the effort of individuals to load upon the CDF so-called "area consensus pet projects," when, in fact, the CDF was already fully loaded and committed to other projects.

Community development and economic development both required high organizational strengths and a substantial energy mass within the central policy groups to have a long-time, on-track effort to raise the economic status of the Tupelo region over a long period. I do not believe that this effort was impossible, but evidence indicates that, with the provincial influence and other cultural and economic disadvantages of the thinkers and the doers, no area in Mississippi has, as of this time, been able to stay the course and continue to have sustained economic growth.

The economic and community development effort must be kept in balance with the growth potential. In my seventy years of experience, the effort always became focused on the community development activities, and the economic development (per income growth) consistently fell into second place and eventually stopped growing. The wealth that is created by economic growth is viewed by most as a personal possession that most people contribute to or use for "pet projects" or leisure-time activities that do not contribute to extending the per-capita income base of the citizens of the area. This action comes and is, in my opinion, successful because it has more motivational opportunities for the individual giving the money to community building projects. These activities and progress also offer more personal opportunities to be involved in activities, to belong, to be recognized, and to experience extended adventures–all of which are major factors in human motivation.

Conversely, economic development, at its best, does not in its present form allow the individual growing the money to get the gratitude and motivation to extend the efforts to grow the per-capita income. It has been my observation that this vision and action do not exist in many areas of our state and the Mid-South to which I have had the privilege to relate.

Another factor that contributes to the lack of progress is the criticism of the economic development push and one that has negative influence against the accumulation and advancement of per-capita income is the sentiment that "You are only interested in the things that are of material value." This idea reaches into the very depths of the most influential people and organizations in each area, and often the objective of material-growth programs is damaged, unfortunately, in the nation's poorest state.

During my career, I became the promotional leader, and to a certain extent, other influential leaders became discouraged to take leadership positions to continue the aggressive economic growth effort. In fact, realistic leaders know as per-capita income of individuals increases, the potential for these individuals to support the many organizations and special fund-raising events increases in the community, thereby enhancing growth and development as well.

This monograph relates to the fifty-two years I spent in the field of economic development. During those years, I learned that there are real issues that each area's leadership must solve if growth is to exist beyond that influenced by inflation. Growth will eventually cease unless a special effort is expended, and a watchdog group is formed to see that the successful effort engendered by the community develops what the group serves.

The "More and Better Jobs" initiative started by CDF in the mid-1950s did more to unify the region and to bring support to CDF from the region than any other project we ever undertook during my administration. The initiative of industrial education by CDF and CRA was started exclusively to inform and educate teachers and administrative officials that economic development was important to schools and, hopefully, encourage the schools to teach more about the free enterprise system and how it works. This program was copied all over the South as a worthwhile program to promote economic development because it filled the need for local people to be employed locally rather than having to migrate to a northern city for employment. Many delegations came to see how the program worked, but few were able to activate and produce the desired results because most leaders who came could not agree on how to set priorities to "create more and better jobs" when returning home. Had it not been for Mr. Morse's leadership and supervision when the Tupelo Plan was adopted, the program would have become just another program or "pet project."

As the Reverend Billy Graham has observed, human nature and people are basically the same worldwide, and Tupelo is no different, so Mr. Morse insisted on a contract for him to manage the programs by selecting a person who worked for him during the formative years of the CDF. The person he selected was Sam Marshall. Most people never knew that Marshall was a contractual employee of Doane Agricultural Institute of St. Louis while starting as the first manager of the CDF economic program.

When I came to CDF in 1956, there was not a true consensus as to where the organization was headed. I was the second executive the local group selected. The first manager employed by CDF was Truman D. Brooks, who had stayed only three years and did a super job but chose another career path to avoid the conflict that was present within the CDF at that time. Mr. Brooks came to the CDF because of the influence of M.C. "Pat" Dougherty when there was an objection from some of the leaders of the area to the employment of a paid professional. Mr. Doane insisted on the meetings being held in the county agent's office since many of these people had a background of rural community living and farming and because, according to Mr. Morse, the long-term economic strength was in the region and not in Tupelo.

One of the policies Mr. Morse stressed was that the leadership in the civic clubs in the small towns, county seats, and the professional agricultural and finance agencies should be involved to the extent of keeping in communication about the planning and events. Mr. Morse also advocated for successful enterprise farmers in dairying and cotton to be used as resource people (rather than the special list of professionals from the various agencies) to present programs of change. His philosophy was that rank-and-file farmers would listen and retain more information from a successful farmer than they would from publications and specialists.

True D. Morse seated on right in a planning session in Washington, D.C. with a task force that drafted the National Rural Development Program in 1956. Harry Martin, Task Force member, standing at left in front row.

County Agent W.J. "Red" Pernell, who had much common sense in application and improvement of practices, saw the logic, and he spent a lot of his time getting successful people in contact with those desiring to improve their living standard and family income. This philosophy proved very successful, and it was adopted by those in other vocations, too. Those evaluating the program and measuring annual progress judged this method of teaching to be very effective. Mr. Morse stayed personally involved for three years as a consultant and later as an interested founder of the philosophy the CDF promoted. I mentioned earlier in my notes that, as a result of his interest in starting the CDF in Tupelo and in Asheville, North Carolina, both program managers (Morris McGough and I) were asked to serve on his task force in Washington, D.C., to help develop the outline for the enactment of the rural development programs under the Eisenhower Administration while Mr. Morse served as undersecretary of agriculture. Mr. Morse was also instrumental in getting CDF visited by several high-level people from the Department of Agriculture, the budget office, and the USDA Graduate School at Silver Springs, Maryland. These visits led to national publicity and leadership assistance that would not have been available otherwise.

Harry Martin and the CDF staff, early 1960s

The Brewer Community Leads the Way

Mr. Morse's plan to organize the rural community in at least three counties was a rescue, with its progressive idea of "more and better jobs" and the need for the larger area to be involved with public input into policy matters related to the future development of the area. There were dozens of examples when assistance was given, but its roots and strong push came from the leader of the Brewer Community, the first RCDC community, which was organized in 1947.

Dozens of families in Brewer, led by Thomas and Eunice Kennedy and Billy and Gladys Flynn, gathered county-wide support and petitioned the Lee County Board of Supervisors to support CDF financially. Mrs. Kennedy had served as a secretary of the RCDC since it was organized. The Brewer action was the result of the progressive spirit of the rural people and their concern for the future of all people in Lee County, especially their children and grandchildren. The Brewer group included the organized black (African American) communities led by Ms. Alice Little, a home demonstration agent.

The Lee County Board of Supervisors began to become a strong partner in economic development, and it was the first one in the state to do so. This movement broke with the prevailing perception that country people were not as smart as those who lived in the city and followed the strong point of Mr. Morse's philosophy that all citizens had to be involved in the growth and development process to reach optimal results in regionalization.

The Kennedys and Flynns, along with many other rural leaders, recognized that the Tupelo business community had been the underwriter of the cost of creating new jobs. This cost amounted to approximately $1,000 per job created between 1947 and 1957. The plan was to create off-farm jobs with Rockwell, Futorian, Super Sagless and other job-creating industries. Most of the people getting the jobs came from a much larger population than that of the city of Tupelo. It was logical that most of the citizens should support the financing and that they should take part in policy decisions regarding the acquisition of new jobs for the area. The Board of Supervisors contributed since its income came from assessments on all property owners in Lee County, in and out of towns. It would be the best way for all citizens to participate in the growth-promotion effort with a much larger group making policy decisions.

As a result of the effort by the Brewer community, U.S. Congressional Representative Jamie Whitten of Mississippi had a picture of the Brewer Community Center and its leaders posted in the Seaman A. Knapp Memorial Arch in the U.S. Department of Agriculture in Washington, D.C. Recognition in this manner was given to those who had accomplished achievements that were of special importance to agriculture and rural development. Such recognition showed the advancement of the influence of the rural area on Tupelo, which was the adjoining county seat.

Some Traditional Problems: Liquor and Gambling

Lee County was dealing with several transitional problems in the last half of the 1950s. Among them was the penetration of a group of gamblers who arrived when they were evicted from Phoenix City, Alabama. With the promise of industrialization and the lax enforcement of liquor prohibition and gambling by local elected law enforcement officers and the lack of interest by the unconcerned judicial system, people began to worry about our local law enforcement upon the arrival of the criminal groups. Several hundred Lee County citizens met on a Sunday afternoon in the old courthouse courtroom to discuss the concept of electing a sheriff, constable, and judges who would stand for more strict law enforcement. Mr. William Beasley was elected president of the group, and I was elected secretary-treasurer. Mr. Beasley was serving as the chairman of CDF, and I had been named by the Junior Chamber of Commerce Lee County's "Young Man of the Year." Our organized group was successful, and the Phoenix City element was forced to move to McNairy County, Tennessee, where Sheriff Buford Pusser became famous for fighting the same criminals. The coming together of our group of concerned citizens is just another example of the power that helped form the future of Lee County. The value of the rural councils, the involvement of all the civic clubs and the many other organized groups, including the churches, were powerful influences on positive change.

A Demographic Profile of the Area

During this time, hundreds of Northeast Mississippi residents migrated to the Midwest to find industrial employment. Historically, Northeast Mississippi had numerous small farms; many families lived with two sources of income, usually from livestock and dairy cows and cotton production. The practice of tenant farming was not as common in Lee County as it was in other parts of Mississippi. Lee County was not formed until 1866, which was the year following the end of the Civil War. Accordingly, there were a few traditions or cultural barriers to be changed. When I came to work in the Lee County's agent's office in 1948, only three farmers in the county owned farms with as many as a thousand acres. Lee County is a small county in area compared to some of the neighboring counties such as Monroe County, which is about twice the size.

Census information for Lee County in the early 1950s showed the population to be about 85% white and 15% black. There were twenty-four separate school districts. The schools were in neighborhoods or communities where usually a country store and a couple of churches were located. Two railroads crossed the county and served nine towns. A few organized villages existed. Hundreds of World War II veterans were enrolled under the GI Bill that sponsored vocational training and educational classes, mostly in high schools.

The oil mill district and other small industries were thriving. The Sunshine Mills Company decided to build grain elevators on South Green Street. The Barber Pure Milk Company Plant was in operation near the intersection of South Gloster Street and South Green Street. The new milk plant bought milk daily from a hundred Grade A dairies in Lee County; the milk was then sent to a receiving station in the Skyline Community. The milk was transferred from the Skyline location to the Birmingham plant where it was processed and packaged into truckloads of fresh milk.

The Spicer-Long Commission Company, which operated a livestock and dairy cattle auction barn in the Northeast area of Tupelo, was in the area called "Shake Rag." Eventually, the area was cleared to make way for the building of a downtown mall. Some three hundred houses and several businesses were removed as part of Mississippi's first urban renewal project. In recent years, the area has been designated as the BancorpSouth Arena. Near this area, but on the south side of Main Street, were the fairgrounds. Each year, the Mississippi-Alabama Fair and Dairy Show was conducted for about a week. In addition to the large number of agricultural and industrial exhibits, there was also a huge carnival. At night there was entertainment in front of the grandstands. One memorable and celebrated performance was by Tupelo native Elvis Presley. The site of the old fairgrounds has now been demolished and is being revitalized as the Fairpark District, consisting of a mixture of government, commercial, and residential buildings.

Recognition of The Supporters of Good Government

After the Phoenix City element was removed to Alcorn County, Mississippi, and McNairy County, Tennessee, the group that led the removal used its influence to elect new public special leaders to the courts and law enforcement in Lee County. The group was composed of these representative leaders and many other community and church leaders from all over Lee County:

Good Government Representatives (Of Record)

District I:

O.O. Cunningham, Baldwyn, Mississippi
J.H. Mabry, Route 3, Baldwyn
John G. Underwood, Guntown
Rob Ford, Box 91, Guntown
Milton M. Messner, Route 1, Guntown
Rev. W.F. Appleby, Guntown

District II:

Bub Epting, Saltillo
Ed Whitten, Euclatubba Road, Saltillo
Hoyt Norris, R.F.D., Saltillo
Herman Jones, Saltillo
Clayborne Magers, Route 3, Baldwyn
Murray Long, Birmingham Road, Saltillo

District III:

Harry A. Martin
Aaron Morgan, Lawhon Junior High School
Felix Black, Black's Department Store
Jack Kelly, 1919 Bella Vista
C.R. Bolton, Box 427, Tupelo
George McLean, Daily Journal

District IV:

Prentiss Harris, Verona
Charlie Monts, Plantersville
Beryle M. Bailey, Box 5, Verona
George Vay Sample, Box 145, Verona
M.B. Pickering, Route 3, Tupelo
Vardaman Robbins, Verona

District V:

Jack Black, Box 36, Shannon
Neil Wise, Box 27, Shannon
V.T. Ivy, Route 1, Shannon
Billy Flynn, Shannon
Arvid R. Cox, Route 2, Shannon
Joe Wiygul, Bank of Nettleton

Executive Committee:

Jack Black- President
W.F. Appleby
Rob Ford- First Vice President
Clayborne Magers
Aaron Morgan- Second Vice President
C.R. Bolton
Harry A. Martin- Secretary-Treasurer
Prentiss Harris
V.T. Ivy

This group of leaders emerged from mostly World War II veterans and church leaders who stepped up to the challenge of economic development plus preservation of the strong legal and moral values that the area had been recognized as having. They had the full support of the group that swept the Lee County Courthouse clean and elected a group of World War II veterans to posts in the courtroom in 1947, the first summer I spent in Lee County. Men like John "Red" Raspberry, Paul Grissom (who lost an arm in military service), and others were not satisfied with the established leadership who did not fight and had remained at home and benefitted while the younger men were away. The ones who stayed at home did not appear to be very enthusiastic about the opportunity for economic growth in jobs and the future of veterans for employment.

During the 15- to 20-year period after the war, agriculture was the first industry mechanized, and large numbers of rural small farm people were replaced. Therefore, a major migration had begun into the large cities where some jobs were available. There were fifty-six organized rural community organizations plus the Community Development Foundation, all unified for community progress underlying the area civic clubs and most elected officials serving in city and county government. The group had cleaned up the bad influence coming in the area to capitalize on the emerging industrial payrolls. The broad base of people involved county-wide and the positive attitude about the future of the area came from the strategic planning with local neighborhood plans plus joining together in major area goals as outlined by Mr. Morse. In his plan was the basic framework to cause, through the Community Development Foundation, what was to become one of the most outstanding rural economic development programs in America and to be recognized intellectually by delegations from most states and more than forty foreign countries which would visit the CDF, Tupelo, and Lee County.

The strong moral and spiritual values, which seemed stronger in the rural areas than in the city, have always had a positive influence on people and sound economic growth in Lee County and the area. This concept was aided by the strong support of church leaders, and the fact that ministers have had a prominent place in the leadership role of this progressive movement, in my opinion. During the past 50 years, the number of organized churches has more than doubled. There are several outstanding examples of the leadership as shown by the American Family Association, a Christian family association led by Donald Wildmon. The formation of the global outreach missionary group led by the Hancock family and many others, including Dr. Sammy Simpson and his wife, has had both national and international influence.

Another outstanding example of strong roots in moral and spiritual value in the local culture was in recent years the formation of the Sanctuary Hospice House, a mission to minister to the people in the last six months of their lives. The influence of this organization has reached four states and hundreds of families, many of whom did not have adequate safe, sanitary, and comfortable living conditions for the last days of their lives. A highly dedicated and a very spiritual staff, executive committee, board of directors, and hundreds of volunteers are involved in rendering the superior facility and loving care for the patients.

Even though the fifties and early sixties were times of depopulation of rural America, the Tupelo Plan proposed by True D. Morse had become extremely effective in causing things to happen in the greater Tupelo area. The large population base made it possible to move from an entirely agricultural-based economy to a more diversified economy where the three big additions were industrial jobs, health care service jobs, and retail and small business service jobs. The increasing family income from manufacturing payrolls supported the above extended economic development. The challenge from the established older industry employers that new industry would challenge and pirate the long-time employees of their firms was overcome when the value of "more and better jobs" proved to be a benefit to the current workforce and was especially important to the future workers who were their children.

The restriction on growth and development that came from the pre-Civil War period in Southern culture promoted by the landlord-tenant system with the landlord also having the store for the workers to get goods and supplies from was still embedded in the culture of Tupelo and most Southern counties. The transition away from that system was successful because CDF had developed among its professional staff a very successful strategy in recruiting new employers who did provide more and better jobs. This strategy, which was kept closely concealed within the group, was extremely effective in seeking outside Fortune 500 companies. In fact, it was so organized that no two people knew which project would be the next to be completed. Assisting with the execution of the plan was the formation of the Community Relations Association (CRA), an agency that was chartered in 1959 to assist CDF in building policies to protect both the companies and the workers. The foundation of the program was initiated first by CDF staff, and when it was determined that CDF could best function with CRA's mission and program outside its doors, the CRA was transferred and became an independent group.

Among the early leaders of CRA was W.L. Wood, a retired milk processor, who was asked, with a little salary and fringe benefits, to manage the program. Ray Purnell of Purnell's Pride Poultry Processing, Robert Sadler of Hunter-Sadler Company, and I spent a lot of time along with George McLean of the *Daily Journal*. Mr. Sadler, Mr. McLean, and I, under the sponsorship of CDF, visited cities in Missouri, Illinois, and North Carolina, seeking input from employers and employees and the National Association of Manufacturers in Washington, D.C. We met with these representatives, and they all advised that we seek the help of a nationally recognized lawyer in the field of labor relations to develop policies that would not conflict with employers' and employees' rights laws. Several workshops led by these experts culminated in the policy and program of CRA. CDF invited outstanding national leaders like Dr. George Heaton, an industrial consultant from Charlotte, North Carolina. From each of these experts, we asked for direction in the areas of recruitment, worker motivation, and the productive record of the manufacturers. As True D. Morse gave the start, CDF drew upon the experts to help us develop one of the 10 best recruiting programs in the nation for attaching industrially diversified manufacturing companies in a town and county. Later, John Osberg of Rockwell, Bill

Pickens of Mooreville, and I became deeply involved with supporting the effort. Mr. Wood served until he retired, and he was succeeded by Vaughn Camp, one of the first employees of Penn Tire and a supervisor, and later by Eddie Richey.

CDF officers, 1998
Left to right: Harry Martin, Chuck Imbler, Mark Ledbetter,
Lewis Whitfield, and John Hicks

Changing the Structure
of Leadership

The structure of leadership had to change to allow an advanced momentum of efforts to promote progress when compared with the prevailing traditional attitude of "wait and see" or "Don't worry; they will come to us." This attitude was the passive one that prevailed among most Southern leaders concerning economic growth and development. Mr. Winkler's introduction of Mr. True D. Morse in the late 1940s would become the pattern for the nation to follow. The assistance of the Fantus Corporation of Chicago, under the leadership of Maurice Fantus and Bob Ady, plus the superior skill of the people of the GM&O, and Joseph Christian and Fred Johnson from Frisco Railroad Company, helped to provide technical advice and consulting service to a responsive leadership group. This group was composed of volunteers, professional staff members, and the consultants without the domination by any one person or group. The mutually agreeable major leadership groups were about to become a structured group with organizational restructuring to prevent a small group from controlling the region's community and economic future.

A small group opposed Jim Hoffman's project. The Chairman, Bill Beasley, who was the owner of the Farmall Tractor dealership that was replacing the mules and horses in power for farm equipment beginning to become motorized in its early stages, gathered a consensus that the project should go forward if the entire community and economic development program were to move to gain international attention for its results. It later did in several ways, but one was the *Wall Street Journal* of March 3, 1994, in an article entitled "Southern Comfort." In 1958, there were 4,500 manufacturing jobs in the county; when I retired from CDF in 2000, there were 18,000 employed in manufacturing, which made Lee County the most industrialized county in Mississippi.

The CDF Adopts
A New Policy

I had been asked in the early 1950s to serve as temporary manager and interim executive of the Community Development Foundation (CDF). I was to fill these positions until the CDF Board of Directors could find a permanent replacement. The CDF in Tupelo was a struggling organization with a $40,000 budget. The foundation was undecided about its policy and mission-pursuit of industrialization or continuation of the agricultural tradition. A new, innovative policy was adopted. Mr. True D. Morse was tasked with recruiting a local leader with a multi-county regional reputation and who would select a leadership team to implement the new policy.

Mr. M.C. "Pat" Dougherty was the founding chairman of the CDF board, and Mr. Sam Marshall was the first CDF executive. Marshall was later replaced by Mr. Truman Brooks. Both men were from outside the community. They were professionals and were not attached to one of the three factions of local leaders who were present in Tupelo. "Mr. Pat," as Mr. Dougherty was known, was respected by hundreds of farm families and many of the bankers in the area.

The agricultural and business leaders in the fourteen counties of Northeast Mississippi administered the Agricultural Credit Agency. This agency had been created during the Franklin Roosevelt Administration during the New Deal to bail out small farmers and save their homes and farms from foreclosure. The Production Credit Association (PCA), under the direction of Mr. Dougherty, approved the money, personal leadership, and conservative financial management for farm families to help them recover from the Great Depression. The activity of the PCA was a major contribution to the state of the economy in Northeast Mississippi, which had been almost exclusively a cotton and dairy farming economy.

In the early 1950s, NBC made a television show on the RCDC Program in our area; later, the "Tomorrow" movie producers asked me to coordinate the assembling of the cast with the exception of the star Robert Duvall, who lived at the Rex Plaza Motel here in Tupelo while the movie, which is still being shown today, was being filmed. I received national recognition for my efforts involving these two endeavors.

CDF's Reaction to Change

The leadership of CDF recognized the change that was occurring and initiated a very aggressive industrial recruitment program that sought employment primarily for men that led to the formation of many companies, such as Futorian, Super Sagless, KI, Rich Toys, National Springs, Horner Boxes, Cushioning Craftsman, and Relaxolounger. These businesses were started not just in Tupelo, but also in locations such as Cedar Hill, Baldwyn, Shannon, and Nettleton. The jobs added to those previously established at Day-Brite and Rockwell, which gave the impression that Lee County was growing at a faster rate than some of the conservative leadership wanted.

The strong labor force complemented the CDF's aggressive recruiting efforts. The area had an available labor force of people with very strong work ethics. Many had milked cows seven days a week and performed duties such as picking cotton. Most of the early industries were very successful in marketing their products from the Tupelo area because of how quickly the markets and population in the South were growing. Tupelo was extremely accessible by truck and rail. Many of the agriculture-based processing, manufacturing, and supplying companies had been established prior to the 1950s, such as International Fertilizers and Minerals, established in 1898; the Carnation Milk Plant, built in the mid-1920s; Purnell's Chicken Processing, begun in the late 1940s; and Mid-South Packers, producers of Southern Belle products. There were many "cut-and-sew" operations, such as Blue Bell, Reeds Manufacturing, Hunter-Sadler Manufacturing, Milam Manufacturing, Lucky Star, and Joyner-Fields, which were operating in this frame as well.

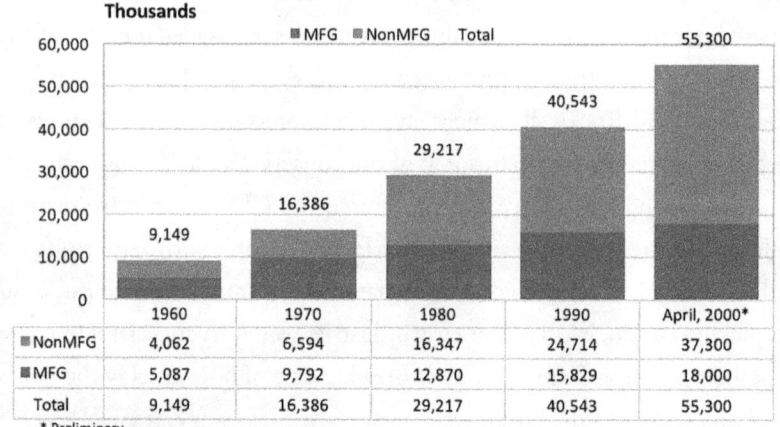

Rural Community Development Council and the CDF

During the 1947 to 1956 period, I had gotten deeply involved with the growth efforts in the region. The factors that helped me were the strategies developed in meetings of the local Rural Community Development Council (RCDC) and CDF between Mr. Dougherty, Mr. McLean, and Mr. Pernell. For the first eight years of the existence of the RCDC and CDF, the county extension agents executed most of the rural and town programs. This situation was true in Lee County where there were RCDC organizations. It was not unusual for two or three thousand people to attend regional field days. These were special events, and visiting delegations such as the president of the Tennessee Valley Authority (TVA), a senator or a congressman would attend. The staff of the Lee County Extension Service was very close to and an integral part of the early CDF program. Because of this, Mr. Pernell was the ex officio member of the board and executive committee of the CDF. I usually attended the meetings with Mr. Pernell to give progress and project reports. We, as Extension agents in Lee and adjoining counties, were deeply involved in programs, plans, and project execution.

Through the Lee County Extension Service, the CDF had direct contact with more than 5,200 farmers and their families through 4-H Clubs, which had more than 600 members, and Demonstration Clubs in more than 20 communities. The staff, through its many organizations, was, at that time, close to the grassroots of the economic and social culture. The staff had an ideal position to know what the people were thinking and what the moods were among the citizens. There were speeches made to groups from all the states and more than forty nations about what makes the area's economic effort work. Books have been written, and there is much speculation, implication, and perception, but few of the inside players have laid out all the facts about the growth of the CDF. Especially missing has been accurate reporting of the struggles within the development agency itself.

Expanding the Reach of CDF

Another outstanding rural development agency was created at the same time as the CDF in Tupelo. This Asheville, North Carolina,-based agency was led by Mr. Morris McGough. Mr. McGough was on Mr. Morse's planning team when the Tupelo Plan was developed. He was often in Tupelo as a consultant in the early days of the program. The expanded effort would be to further diversify and extend the influence of the CDF into a larger region. CDF was chartered with Mr. Morse as its advisor and the stipulation that its primary geographic reach should be 50 miles in every direction.

As a young professional, I was privileged to work with a broad base of architects and experts on the future direction of the region's engine to drive the economy, which would become a national model. The input and experience of professionals who represented the Gulf, Mobile and Ohio (GM&O) Railroad Company and the Frisco Railroad Company should be properly recognized. Mr. T.T. Martin, vice president of GM&O in Mobile, Alabama, and other high-level officials went well beyond expectations to help teach me the art of industrial recruitment. They helped the CDF develop the first industry-oriented information publication that became a valuable tool in the CDF'S recruitment arsenal. Mr. Joe Christian of Collierville, Tennessee, who was employed by the Frisco Railroad Company, shared knowledge and experience confidentially with us and helped CDF find dozens of prospects to build plants in the region. Mr. Christian is active in Tupelo-Burlington Railroad contracts even today. Another strong member of our team was the Fantus Company of Chicago, Illinois. This company offered excellent service for our recruitment of Fortune 500 companies.

Mr. Hoffman's Stop in Tupelo

In early March 1958, a decade after the establishment of Day-Brite Lighting Company and Rockwell Manufacturing Company in Tupelo, Mississippi, someone reported that an automobile had pulled into Mr. Walter Harrell's Gulf Service Station, which was located on the southeast corner of Main Street and Green Street in Tupelo. Little did we know that the routine stop in March 1958 at the Gulf Station would be a prominent turning point in the economic growth history of Tupelo, Lee County, and Northeast Mississippi. The subsequent actions resulting from that occurrence would change the economic atmosphere of the region and be an example that was used to lead the way to a national revamping of rural programs originating in Washington, D.C.

The man in the automobile was Mr. Jim Hoffman, leader of the Mansfield Tire Organization in Mansfield, Ohio. I never knew who was at Walter's service station except him, but I do know that Jim Hoffman was impressed with the generosity and hospitality he enjoyed while traveling on U.S. 78 from Atlanta to Memphis.

Mr. Hoffman was so impressed with the hospitality he had experienced that he decided to locate a tire manufacturing plant in Lee County. He called and was connected to J.M. "Ikey" Savery, chairman of CDF Industrial Recruiting Committee, and the process began. Ultimately, and after much debate, they located the plant on South Green Street in Tupelo. Let me hasten to say that it was not the location of Penn Tire that changed the direction of economic growth, but rather, it was the change in the policy of the CDF Board that caused it.

Mr. Dougherty had resigned because of a severe heart attack that limited his schedule. His resignation brought on a change in CDF Board policy and leadership. Elected to replace Mr. Dougherty was Mr. William "Bill" Beasley, a young farm machinery and truck dealer who had established himself and his business as a regional multi-county leader.

You may be wondering why Jim Hoffman's "pit stop" in Tupelo was so important. Mr. Hoffman did not stop gathering information about building a manufacturing facility in Tupelo. The timing of this stop was coincidental with the economic and political situation that was about to undergo positive changes. The area leaders, especially in Tupelo, were uneasy with the rapidly growing economy and its effect on companies with many minimum-wage employees. This uneasiness was one of the CDF's first challenges with its new growth-development policy.

The professional leadership of the CDF was well-trained with the marketing skills required to recruit major industries and was being successful in its endeavors. The leadership had superb support from some of the most experienced professionals in the nation, including those with the GM&O Railroad (now Kansas City Southern) and the Frisco Railroad (now the Burlington Northern). Mayor J.P. Nanney was active in bringing the Day-Brite Lighting Company to Tupelo in 1946. Mr. Julius Berry, who served as local project chairman, and the Fantus Company, the most successful industrial location service and location agency, brought Rockwell Manufacturing to Tupelo in 1948. These two companies, established immediately after World War II and employing primarily male workers from the 60 RCDC communities, demonstrated the wisdom of aggressive industrial development efforts as World War II veterans returned home and became available to enter the workforce.

The industrial committee had gained the full support of the Lee County Board of Supervisors and a large group of rural leaders with the RCDC. In 1948, Mr. John A. "Red" Rasberry, a candidate for the office of chancery clerk, led a complete sweep of county government elected officials. Most of the newly elected officials were World War II veterans. The many civic club members touched the tempo and would provide the guiding direction and active leadership that followed. Each year, community goals were set and submitted to the area's council. They were to strive to reach while also undertaking one long-time regional goal that was selected by the entire council. This goal-setting process is what set the Tupelo Plan on the road to be very productive and aggressive in advancing the economy. There were organized communities all over the South, but this was the first time a coordinated goal-setting was a multiple community activity and achievement. This organization of communities mobilized all tools available for regional development and concentrated regional leadership, reaching to the grassroots of the area's culture.

The most commonly regional goal adopted was "more and better jobs for us and our children." Reaching this goal required many coaching sessions, and the CDF job took days and evenings every week maintaining the RCDCs. It was a job that most people did not want. For example, in the first three years that I worked at CDF, I spent no weekday evenings at home. Rather, I was on the road to a hundred meetings per month.

My predecessor at CDF, Mr. Truman D. Brooks, was a dedicated organizer and left big shoes to fill. Mr. True D. Morse was our continuing source of professional knowledge along with Mr. Morris McGough, who was associated with Mr. Doane and later took over the North Carolina project. Little did we know at this time that Mr. Morse and Mr. Harold Kaufman of the Social Science Research Center at Mississippi State University were directing us towards a foundation that could motivate large groups of community leaders to work together to achieve regional goals. Dr. Kaufman and his group recorded the progress and did social science research that helped in evaluating the program results.

The Importance of the Early Gasoline Service Stations

Jim Hoffman's first stop at Walter Harrell's Gulf Station was in the business center of Tupelo and at a location which had one of the highest traffic counts in the area. There was a Standard Oil Station across the street that John A. "Red" Rasberry operated. It was the location from which he launched his political campaign seeking the office of chancery clerk to sweep the occupants out of the Lee County Courthouse in 1947. He was successful. On the southwest corner of Main and Green was another service station that had the motto, "We doze but never close." It was overseen by "Red" Lawhon.

These service stations were more than a place where you could fill up your vehicle with gasoline. One could also get the water, oil, and air in the tires checked, as well as get the windshield cleaned. These stations, where local and transit travelers stopped, were in effect the hospitality centers of a city. Cold drinks, cigarettes, and packaged snacks were available to a traveler, as well as the most available restrooms in town. The owners like Harrell, Rasberry, and Lawhon were more than service station operators; they were well-informed and respected citizens and operated almost as a branch of the local Chamber of Commerce. They gave out brochures and road maps and shared area points of interest with their customers. These local leaders had the same public interest and spirit as leaders of the 60 rural community development communities in Lee and the surrounding counties. This pure spirit was to be found in Pontotoc, Union, Tippah, Alcorn, Tishomingo, Itawamba, Monroe, and Chickasaw counties. At this time in rural Mississippi, the operators of cafes, restaurants, and other small businesses, such as the small Maw & Paw grocery and farm supply stores were respected, church-going community leaders.

I do not know if Jim Hoffman encountered others as he traveled through the area, but he was impressed with his stop at Walter's Gulf Service Station. The employees had made a thorough inspection of his car, and they had expressed genuine appreciation for having the opportunity to service his car. Jim Hoffman is reported to have asked about the air pressure in his tires, including his spare tire. The attendant reported that they had all been checked and were okay. Little did the station workers and Walter know that Jim was president of a major automobile tire manufacturing company in Mansfield, Ohio. Jim appreciated the service station people's knowledge and understanding of automobiles. There was no way at this time to know that Mr. Hoffman's visit would eventually culminate in the expansion and broadening of the scope of the Tupelo Plan. The expanded effort would be to further diversify and extend the influence of the CDF into a larger region. You may recall that CDF was chartered with Mr. Morse advising that its primary geographic area should be 50 miles in every direction.

Harry A. Martin, "Best Man" *Lee County Courier*, 2000

Mr. Harry A. Martin sitting in the rocking chair presented to him by Governor Kirk Fordice during a banquet honoring Mr. Martin's retirement in 2000.

Mr. Harry A. Martin and Mrs. Agnes N. Martin visiting Sydney, Australia

Mr. Harry A. Martin with Governor Haley Barbour 2010

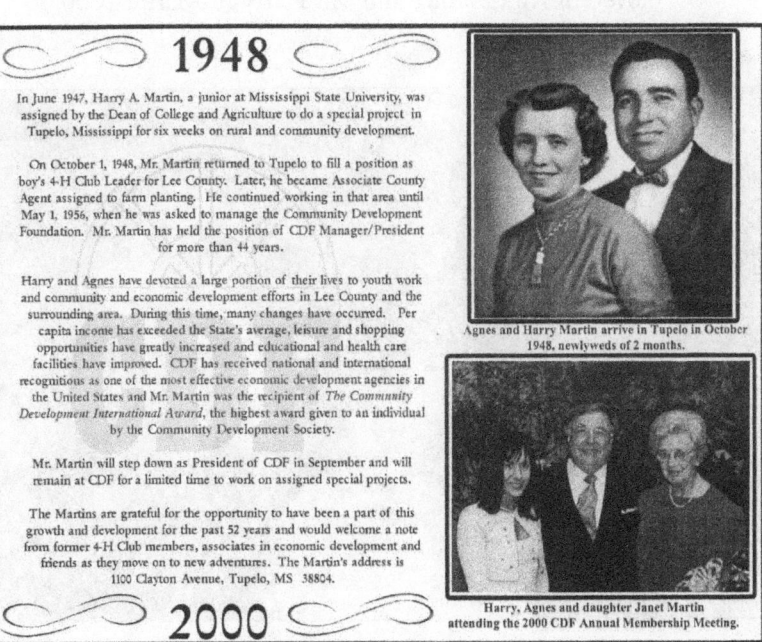

1948

In June 1947, Harry A. Martin, a junior at Mississippi State University, was assigned by the Dean of College and Agriculture to do a special project in Tupelo, Mississippi for six weeks on rural and community development.

On October 1, 1948, Mr. Martin returned to Tupelo to fill a position as boy's 4-H Club Leader for Lee County. Later, he became Associate County Agent assigned to farm planting. He continued working in that area until May 1, 1956, when he was asked to manage the Community Development Foundation. Mr. Martin has held the position of CDF Manager/President for more than 44 years.

Harry and Agnes have devoted a large portion of their lives to youth work and community and economic development efforts in Lee County and the surrounding area. During this time, many changes have occurred. Per capita income has exceeded the State's average, leisure and shopping opportunities have greatly increased and educational and health care facilities have improved. CDF has received national and international recognitions as one of the most effective economic development agencies in the United States and Mr. Martin was the recipient of *The Community Development International Award*, the highest award given to an individual by the Community Development Society.

Mr. Martin will step down as President of CDF in September and will remain at CDF for a limited time to work on assigned special projects.

The Martins are grateful for the opportunity to have been a part of this growth and development for the past 52 years and would welcome a note from former 4-H Club members, associates in economic development and friends as they move on to new adventures. The Martin's address is 1100 Clayton Avenue, Tupelo, MS 38804.

2000

Agnes and Harry Martin arrive in Tupelo in October 1948, newlyweds of 2 months.

Harry, Agnes and daughter Janet Martin attending the 2000 CDF Annual Membership Meeting.

Harry Martin and the Community Development Foundation

Governor Kirk Fordice and Mr. Harry A. Martin 2000

Mrs. Agnes N. Martin, Janet M. Martin, and Harry A. Martin

Mr. Harry A. Martin received the Mississippi State University College of Agriculture and Life Sciences Alumni Achievement Award 2016-2017 on April 8th, 2017.

Standing left to right:
First Row: Jim Collins (1985-86), Harry A. Martin, President (1956-2000), C. V. Imbler (1989-1990), Jim High (1977-79), Guy Gravlee (1963-64), Lewis Whitfield (1991-92), Irvin "Buddy" Prude (1986-87), Guy Mitchell III (1987-88), Bill Vanover (1998-99), Jeff Barber (1999-2001).
Second Row: L. E. Gibens (1982-83), Jim Ingram (1996-97), Charles Johnston (1984-85), Marion Cagle (1973-74), Jack Reed, Sr. (1968-69), John A. Rasberry (1970-71), Felix Black (1962-63), James Hugh Ray (1975-76), Jim Threldkeld (1972-73), Billy Wheeler (1981-82), Gray Megginson (1980-81), Larry Kirk (2001-2002).
Third Row: Tom Bailey (1969-70), John W. Smith (1993-94), Richard Hill (1979-80), Mark Ledbetter (1990-91), Bruce Smith (1995-96), Ed Neelly III (1988-89), Robert C. Leake (1971-72), Len Pegues (1983-84), Aubrey Patterson (1994-95).

Past Chairmen Deceased

M. C. "Pat" Dougherty (1948-1956) | W. M. Beasley, Sr. (1957-1962) | Bill Dunlap (1964-65, 1967-68) | J. M. Thomas, Jr. (1965-1966) | Harry Rutherford (1966-1967) | Hoyt Payne (1974-1975) | Todd Agnew (1976-1977)

3Qs Harry Martin
president emeritus of CDF

Harry Martin is president emeritus of the Tupelo-based Community Development Foundation, which celebrates its 60th anniversary this month. Martin started working for the CDF at its start, retiring from the economic development group in 2000 at the age of 75. Business Editor spoke to Martin at the First Friday event.

Q: How did you get involved with CDF?

A: It was in 1947 and I was a student at Mississippi State and my professor sent me to Tupelo. I got six weeks to write a report about this new idea that was going on. I never planned to work here.
And then they called me to work 60 years ago for the staff. I was the extension agent for eight years.
The CDF had no money, with a $28,000 budget and two employees and I didn't think it was going to work.
But I enjoyed the work ... I spent 52 years of my life with the CDF.

Q: Did you ever think Tupelo and Lee County would be in the position it's in economically?

A: I had no idea we'd be here. Back then, the three banks in Tupelo had $20 million in deposits between them. We had 5,200 farmers milking cows and making 30,000 bales of cotton. Our per capita income – it wasn't very good at all. We also had issues with our educational levels.
But we've made quite a lot of progress since then.

Q: There have been many achievements in the last 60 years. Any one accomplishment that stands out?

A: There are so many moments and people that would be considered highlights.
The secret is that-we had hundreds of people who made huge contributions.
Our tendency is to have people like us get up and talk about what we did, but in reality, there were many, many more people behind the scenes who worked just as hard.
I think one of the biggest things we did was back in 1959. We had 4,500 jobs in industry in town, which was followed by an explosion in those jobs, growing to 18,000.
Those kinds of jobs paid 1½ times to 1¾ better, which meant there was more discretionary income to put into education, cultural activities, etc., that we didn't have.
And I think the water issue, too, was big. If we hadn't solved that, then it would have shut the town down. Without water, there'd be no Toyota.

Northeast Mississippi Daily Journal article September 2008

The Lasting Influence of Mr. Hoffman's Visit

Although Jim Hoffman's visit to Tupelo, Mississippi, did not directly or immediately contribute to economic growth in Northeast Mississippi, he later brought a project to the CDF that would affect Mr. Morse's Tupelo Plan in a positive way. Mr. Hoffman's project made the local leaders look at outdated and provincial ways of thinking. That helped the community to raise its vision and ambition, which resulted in a shift in the way things were implemented, especially in the areas of advancing and marketing the advantages of the Mid-South's people and natural resources. The proposal put forth by Mr. Hoffman was to build an automobile tire manufacturing plant in Tupelo that was technologically and capital-oriented and a departure from the labor-based manufacturing that rural America, including the Tupelo area, had revolved around and depended upon during the first half of the 20th century. The labor cost proposed by Mr. Hoffman would be less than 10% of the total tire production cost, compared to the labor-intensive agricultural and poultry processing, which, by industrial classification, were always on the lower scale of wages and had usually attracted mostly female employees. Other plants and operators in the emerging furniture manufacturing industry had a labor cost amounting to 40% or more of the total cost of production.

In retrospect, I do not believe that the sizeable group of leaders helping Mr. Hoffman was aware of what was going to happen positively in the area with this project. As I look back, I recall the influence of the supervisors of the third and fourth districts in Lee County. Mr. Kyle Brown, Mr. Charlie Cain, Mr. Clifton Pettigrew, and Mr. "Buck" Lipford were instrumental in the start of what was to become a key part of the solution and change that was before the CDF and the area. These four men presented a case for positive change and a new direction and increased the effectiveness of regional leaders. As a result, a close-knit relationship formed at the time between the board of supervisors and the CDF. This partnership included members of both the black and white leadership of all the area Rural Community Development Corporation clubs (RCDC), which helped to make it a powerful group. This new arrangement made the area more competitive and very successful in its economic growth. Action could be expedited with new development prospects interested in the Northeast Mississippi community.

Additional Positive Influence of the CDF

Jim Hoffman's proposal brought to the table the issue of whether the community would continue to seek industry to promote more or stop the effort. It also brought up several other issues that would positively influence the future character and cooperation of the CDF. The relatively rural cultural life of the region needed the introduction of more advanced technology and development. It needed to continue advanced learning opportunities through the pioneering establishment of an early relationship with Itawamba Junior College (now Itawamba Community College), the University of Mississippi (Ole Miss) and Mississippi State College (now Mississippi State University). His proposal was helpful in this period of community growth and solidified the support of public groups such as the board of supervisors, as well as city and regional groups such as CRA, Three Rivers, Tennessee Valley Authority, and later, the Appalachian Regional Commission (ARC). Some supporting state groups were the Mississippi Research and Development Center (R&D Center) and the Balance Agriculture with Industry (BAWI) Board, now the Mississippi Development Authority (MDA). A new national model rushed by TVA and the SECDA accelerated the momentum of professional information and leadership in the community development movement at the time.

CDF was fortunate to have had William "Bill" Beasley serving as chairman. Bill was a World War II veteran who was seriously injured when his Navy fighter airplane crashed into the sea. He had recovered when the odds were against him. A strongly dedicated Christian, Bill was respected by both cultures – the country folks and city people. The unifying of regional leadership was growing daily.

Mr. Beasley's local International Harvester dealership was a progressive farm equipment and truck marketer with not only regional but also state and national success. He gained the confidence and respect of the people with his success in changing methods and techniques. He was aware that he must not set himself socially and economically above his customers and friends, and he was respected for his experience and acquaintance with individuals in state and regional positions. He would always take advantage of and attend management training and adopt current successful practices. He had a relationship with one of the most progressive agricultural technology companies in the world. He was a detail-oriented person and could analyze difficult situations without getting too involved personally, and he was extremely objective.

Jim Hoffman's project was to help build and operate a modern auto tire manufacturing plant in Tupelo that was similar to the one in Mansfield, Ohio. The project was actively opposed by several influential leaders in Tupelo because of the closeness of the "Tupelo Leadership" group and the fact that this central group was divided when, historically, the group was usually together before it offered support for projects under consideration. Some of the most effective people became neutralized in influence when it came to shifting from local projects to more regionalized efforts. The leadership of Mr. Beasley and others in the Tupelo Plan movement emerged as the ones who would stand by and support regional development. The project was only a small part of the issue at hand; the greater issue was whether Tupelo would remain as provincial as most places in the South were. One thing necessary for a major change is the implementation of something entirely different that requires much detailed strategy that promotes a higher level of thinking and approach to doing things that would visualize and promote the new future economic development achievement. Another necessity is a policy that uses the highest level of professional assistance and keeps the local business leaders and community volunteer leaders involved in a tight partnership often dominated in the past by a few sideline conservative individuals.

A World-Class Dairy Cattle Business

Lee County and the region had previously depended mostly on agriculture and the manufacturing of agricultural products such as what was provided by the International Mineral and Chemical Plant in North Tupelo. The cottonseed processing plant and oil mill were just two blocks south of Walter Harrell's service station. Purnell's Pride frozen food lockers and poultry processing was a developing business that employed many chicken pluckers and farm broiler production workers. This time was the period when Barber Pure Milk Company in Birmingham purchased the last of the large Grade A milk processors, Carr-Meyers Dairy, located on the lot north of the Rex Plaza and next to the Savings Oil Station on North Gloster Street.

Mr. Gale Carr, a Missouri native who had been working to improve the dairy cattle industry at the Shelby County penal farm in Memphis, Tennessee, was employed by the three local banks to come to Lee County to continue the promotion of the economics of the dairy industry here. Mr. Carr was to continue work done by other dairy specialists employed by the banks that led to the location of Carnation Milk Company, reported as the first condensing of milk south of the Mason-Dixon Line states in the mid-1920s. His first major technical project was to start the use of artificial insemination of dairy cows. The first time this project was accomplished in Mississippi was in 1941, which was several years ahead of the Agricultural Experiment Station at Mississippi State. The Tupelo Area Artificial Insemination Association (TAAIA) was one of several organizations Mr. Morse recommended be consolidated with CDF in its charter along with the Lee

County Jersey Cattle Club and the Tupelo Marketing Association (a group that promoted the production of strawberries, blackberries, sweet potatoes, and crimson clover seed).

There was another major project by Mr. Carr, with assistance from Mr. Pernell; Mr. Dougherty; and Mr. Rex Reed, a pioneer breeder of registered Jersey cattle and the manager of Forest Hills Farm; and Mr. Ray Robison, father of Dr. Rud Robison. Forest Lake was where Ballard Park and Oren Dunn Museum are now. The three bankers and PCA, headed by Mr. Dougherty, provided financing for many of the dairy products including the financing of the twenty-one head of Jerseys imported from the Isle of Jersey off the coast of England in 1947. The twenty females (heifers) were sold to 4-H Club members from all sections of Lee County at a cost of $1,000 each. The male (bull) was placed with the TAAIA, and each insemination cost between five and six dollars. TAAIA Bull Stud and Lab was located on Thomas Street, where Thomas Street School, the Tupelo Post Office, and the Hancock Company office are currently.

The Lee County Jersey Cattle Club later won the national award on three occasions for its outstanding work in breeding and in showing registered Jerseys. I was assigned by Mr. Pernell to work with the 4-H members and their registered calves. We showed the animals in all seven district shows in Mississippi and in Memphis at the Mid-South Fair. A select group of winners was transported by rail car to Columbus, Ohio, for the national show, and many blue and purple ribbons were won. One of the groups was on the road for six weeks in the shows in the state. This animal won every championship except one at the Newton Mississippi Dairy Show.

Mr. Gale Carr was brought to Lee County by a grant from three banks to help promote a world-class dairy business. The strategy was to diversify farming and ensure a year-round income for farmers to supplement the major cash crop at that time. With 5,200 families in the county classified as a dairy and/or cotton producers and Mr. Carr's leadership, there were over a hundred dairy-producing farms with the emphasis on breeding Jersey cattle for show and milk. The Lee County Jersey Cattle Club was a regular winner of the annual national award that promoted registered Jerseys and was presented by the American Jersey Cattle Club of Columbus, Ohio. The breeding and sale of registered stock was profitable and provided additional income for the farm families. People came from all over the nation to buy registered Jersey stock.

The Lee County Extension Service staff and all the other extension service workers in adjoining counties were extremely active in the economic development and growth of Northeast Mississippi. Once again, Mississippi State had a large part of the development of the dairy industry by having workshops, shows, and registered Jersey sales on a regular schedule. Mr. Higgins and his assistant, Mr. Arlis Anderson, were very involved doing training sessions for 4-H Club members.

During this time, two local businesses were established. The Spicer-Long Commission Company was formed just where the north part of the BancorpSouth Coliseum is, and it was advertised as the largest dairy cow auction in America. The same team built a local packing plant that processed cattle and hogs. The plant was first named Mid-South Packers, but the name was later changed to Southern Belle. Lee and Pontotoc counties dominated the dairy cattle shows throughout the Mid-South. Breeders would compete in shows as far away as Columbus, Ohio. The principal leaders in the promotion of wealth building were the USDA State Agricultural Agencies and the Farm Credit Administration. They provided loans for crop production, livestock, cattle, and farmland purchase and ownership. The local Tupelo banks had limited capital, with about $20 million in deposits in the early 1950s.

Usually, the USDA agencies would not support the introduction of change, but under the influence of Mr. Dougherty and county agent, Red Pernell, the CDF was not only fully supported, but much of the area and organizational Morse Plan strategy was led by these dozens of workers. In the 1950s, the CDF had only one-half of the employees it has today. I was privileged to work with a broad base of architects of the future direction of the region's economy. The input and experience of the professionals who represented the GMO and Frisco Railroads have never been properly recognized locally. T.T. Martin, vice president of GM&O in Mobile, Alabama, and other high-level officials went well beyond what was anticipated to help in teaching me the art of industrial recruitment.

Additionally, they helped us develop the first industry-oriented facts information publication that became a valuable tool in CDF's recruitment of both railroad and industrial leaders. Joe Christian of Collierville, Tennessee, who worked for the Frisco Railroad, shared his knowledge and experience confidentially with us and dozens of prospects to be sought by CDF. Another strong team member was the Fantus Company in Chicago, Illinois, which was the most successful recruiting industrial locating and consulting company in the world during the 1950-2000 period.

Imported Heifers from the Isle of Jersey

Development of the National Rural Development Act

An appointment by the President in 1956 gave the authority that Mr. Morse needed as the most nationally recognized instructional leader specializing in rural development. Planners were serving us under the secretary of agriculture in the Eisenhower Administration when he asked Morris, me, and a dozen or so others to serve on a national task force to develop what was to become the National Rural Development Act. This legislation was to become the facilitator of preserving the economic and social values of the rural community. These values had become a part of the new national quality of life standards. It expanded the Farmers Home Administration (FHA) that led in home liens, small farm loans, loans to rural water associations and rural grants for industrial and commercial economic development which connected with Mr. Morse's basic philosophy as the author of the Tupelo Plan in 1947, and with the powerful position of Representative Jamie Whitten and Senator John Stennis. Many of the federal and state regional programs were implemented because of one committee's recommendation of national needs. The region received special attention when applying for federal program assistance to the benefit of the region. One was the Town Creek Flood Control Program for which Mr. Dougherty pushed so hard, which was later called "Mr. Dougherty's Dam Project." Another result was the formation of the Appalachian Regional Commission that has funded dozens of growth projects for Northeast Mississippi, including part of the regional water supply district. One of the greatest benefits was creating the four-lane on Highway 78 from Memphis, Tennessee, to Birmingham, Alabama, and the construction of Mississippi Highway 6 from Batesville, Mississippi, to Tupelo, Mississippi. Dozens of industrial access roads, such as Coley, Cliff Gookin, and Eason were constructed. These roads were built to improve the flow of traffic from the rural area markets – local, regional, and national.

Recruiting Mr. Al Krueger

The first part of the 1960s was very challenging. There were few examples nationwide of successful communities concerning new job development and area-wide success stories in economic development and growth. There were many examples of organized community strategies for self-gratification and "pet project" success stories. I first noticed the inadequacy of economic recruitment when I came to work at CDF. I was in Green Bay, Wisconsin, working with Mr. Al Krueger on a possible plant location in Lee County, and after I had completed the presentation, he was complimentary and walked to a storage closet in the company conference room where we were meeting. He opened the door, and inside the closet must have been information from at least a hundred organizations and communities, which he referred to as mostly junk. They contained no detailed facts and economic plant management assets and liabilities that were of a comparative value as to where the location of a plant should be to achieve the best productivity and climate for success.

I had selected two possible sites for his plant, prepared a site plan, and developed an estimated budget for financing the plant, and listed two possible methods of financing with consideration of tax exemptions and other local incentives. Of special interest to Mr. Al Krueger was the availability and work ethic of the workers. I had prepared information about the loyalty, work ethic, and dependability of the area's workers and the history of the exact rates of wages and fringe benefits of production and office workers. I included the changes in the past three years, with the details of increases in such a manner that Mr. Al Krueger could project the cost of labor for his new plant.

On the flight back to Tupelo, I listed the positive parts of our presentation. I did not let it bother me that we had not yet developed the ability to do a custom-made presentation for each client. We at CDF expedited the effort to develop a staff that had the research composition and building and site development capacity to make CDF's presentation always superior to our competitors. We discovered that the location process had to be confidential, not only in the community but also within the organized CDF staff. I noted early in my career that the most beneficial and professional presentations to the clients were the ones developed by the qualified staff workers. Immediately upon receiving a request, staff workers would be supportive and give the request a very high production priority and delivery.

Industry location success was related to factors that most communities are not able to manage. I noticed that Mr. Guy Nerren, president of the Huntsville, Alabama, Development Authority, was also successful. After exchanging information and developing a professional relationship, we both gained competitiveness and were loyal to prospects. The key to this success was a group of highly informed professionals with a record of integrity, honesty, and accuracy in presenting state and local information. Of necessity was an organization that had a strong financial component with a record of guaranteed commitments and references of contractual location projects, including the proper assessment of local and state government participation.

One important rule is to never present a weak proposal to a client; it must be solid and backed financially by all agencies involved. Because of our attention to detail, we had experience and could read the attitudes of local decision-makers. We had watched ambitious marketing by experienced groups that were caught short on the delivery of promised incentives. Mr. Nerren and I got manufacturing plants when others had failed to perform on promises and commitments. Another key element of our marketing was to never speak negatively against a competing community that was in the race for the project.

Manufacturing Employment Sought for Area Workers

In the 1950s, the upholstered furniture and component parts businesses got under way. Mr. Morris Futorian had begun in New Albany and expanded into Tupelo and Okolona. Horner Boxes was built on South Green Street. Cushioning Craftsman, which was located on the corner of Green and Whitaker Streets, was owned by two German brothers, the Newells. Cushioning Craftsman processed horse and hog hair to use as padding for furniture. Unfortunately for the Newells, a company, Sheller-Globe based in Iowa, developed a chemical and a new process to make polyurethane designed first for the Ford Motor Company. This innovation revolutionized the padding and composition of upholstered furniture and many other products. Local merchants had invested $150,000 in Super Sagless Springs with the Banks family to manufacture hardware for the developing furniture industry as promoted by Morris Futorian.

Day-Brite Lighting and Rockwell Manufacturing were in full production with hundreds of people employed. The GM&O Railroad purchased twenty-one acres of land on South Green Street from the old People's Bank and developed it into an industrial park. The railroad built a flood-control levee around the land and installed a large pumping station in the southeast corner which joined its mainline. Malone and Hyde Company built a major food-distributing center. Wallace Johnson of Memphis built a wholesale building material facility next to the GM&O industrial area.

Tradition

The main players on the court as community leaders at this time were Bill Beasley, as the chairman of the CDF; James Ballard as the mayor; Frank Riley as the city attorney; J.C. Whitehead, president of Bank of Tupelo (who had succeeded J.P. Nanney as president of the bank); and Ray Purnell of Purnell's Pride Poultry Processing. Others playing leadership roles were Todd Agnew of Mid-South Packers; Tom Bailey of the Southern Bell Telephone Company; Jack Reed, Sr., of Reed's; Hoyt Payne of Community Federal Savings & Loan; Johnny Osberg, manager of Rockwell Manufacturing; Cliff Eason, president of The People's Bank & Trust Company; Gordon Houston of Borden's Milk; Ray Aycock, manager of the Tupelo Water & Light Department; Guy Mitchell, Jr., attorney for CDF; Felix Black of Black's Department Store; Dr. A.N. Wilson, city alderman at-large; George McLean, publisher of the *Daily Journal*; Bill Dunlap of Dunlap Pontiac and Cadillac; John A. "Red" Rasberry, chancery clerk; Charlie Cain, county supervisor; Kyle Brown, county supervisor; Clifton Pettigrew, county supervisor; Calvin Turner, county supervisor; Buck Lipford, county supervisor; James M. Savery, chairman of CDF's Industrial Committee and owner of Savery's Insurance; Bill Reed, manager of Blue Bell Manufacturing; W.P. Mitchell, attorney on the board of supervisors and owner of a law firm; Bill McClure of McClure Furniture Company; J.E. Staub and Travis Staub of Fulton, principals of J.E. Staub & Company (now JESCO); T.T. Martin, vice president of the GM&O Railroad in Mobile, Alabama; Jim Crowe, Mississippi Valley Gas Company; L.D. Hancock, Hancock Company; Norris Caldwell, Caldwell's Furniture and Appliances; Pete Albritton of Verona, Mississippi State University's Experiment Station; Gartrell Milam, Milam Manufacturing Company; and J.M. Thomas of Leake & Goodlett, Inc.

The involvement of the extension service, county, district, state, and national organizations, along with the leadership of other federal agencies, has not been adequately recognized for the contributions they made. These professionals in the county and home demonstration offices in Lee, Itawamba, Monroe, Prentiss, Pontotoc, and Chickasaw counties were at that time, along with the State Department of Vocational Education and the high schools of the area, all supporters of the professional leadership for the early RCDC organizations. I served with W.J. Pernell on the Lee County Extension staff as an assistant and later as associate county agent for eight years, and we were daily involved with the Tupelo Plan planning with Mr. Morse, Mr. Dougherty, Mr. Pernell, and Mr. McLean.

The CDF organization was born in the county agent's office, which was housed on the first floor of the City-County Building. The CDF office was connected to the county agent's office. We attended and, in most cases, arranged the program for the RCDC. I was asked to come to the CDF on May 1, 1956, after having served eight years with the extension service. Mr. Pernell and I attended the CDF board meetings in the Blue Room of the Hotel Tupelo as ex officio members, so I have had an inside seat at all activities of the formation of the Tupelo Plan and the CDF.

The CDF started with a $30,000 annual budget, and it had grown to $38,000 in 1956. There was one full-time staff member (Elsie Francis) and a part-time staff member whose job was to answer Chamber of Commerce mail and other miscellaneous duties. The CDF board meetings from 1948 to 1956 were mostly "gripe sessions" and a place for several of the seventeen members of the board to complain about moving from the agenda of the old Chamber of Commerce to the new CDF as outlined by Mr. Morse's Tupelo Plan. Since I had ten years of federal and state retirement benefits earned, my eight years and two years of military service, I had no interest in changing jobs. Eventually, Mr. Dougherty got me to agree to keep my affiliation with the MSU Extension Service for a year until the group selected the new CDF manager/executive. I agreed.

Tradition: A Roadblock to Progress

Tradition is the largest roadblock to progress. There were many more people, even though they were not on the Board of the CDF, who supported each side of the two issues that would change the economic and cultural composition of the Lee County area for years to come. The issue was whether the CDF would pursue the location of Penn Tire and other Fortune 500 companies of national and international origin. Penn Tire was projected to employ 1,000 people. Some of the older established individuals and business and industry leaders contended that the 4,500 jobs in manufacturing in Lee County were all we needed at the time. Outside capital, technology, and new citizens were not good ideas in the view of many local people. There was a concern that the local power structure would be challenged eventually. Another group, mostly made up of World War II veterans, argued that we needed more and better-paying jobs for two reasons. First, they would give under-employed people a chance to advance, and secondly, there were hundreds of veterans having to leave their native area and homes for industrialized cities of the Midwest and North to seek employment. The employers in the area offered jobs mostly to females, but, traditionally, the man was the principal bread-earner in the family. This policy had already resulted in the relocation and migration of about 20,000 people from the farms and immediate trade area to other sections from this immediate geographic area for jobs.

This happening had resulted in a situation where good parents got together in dozens of communities and worked hard to help and support the effort of bringing in better assistance and support to the effort of bringing in more and better jobs. Most of the financial support for this effort came from a few businesses in Tupelo. As a result, this small group was able to control the development policy. Sometimes, potentially good employers were kept from coming to the area to give employment to the large labor force.

CDF's Industrialization Strategy

The industrialization strategy that was used between 1950 and 2000 was not the traditional initiative advocated by national economic developers. The secret came from the vast experience of senior officials of the GM&O and Frisco railroads, key members of TVA's staff, namely, Ralph Carnathan, who was Gary's brother, both of whom were natives of Palmetto, Lee County; Carol Marsalis, education consultant; and Jack Fortenberry, information and technology consultant of TVA. The lead national consultant was a representative of the Fantus Company in Chicago, Robert M. "Bob" Ady. The key CDF staff personnel were Betti Scott, Nick Chandler of the Council of Governments, Barbara Smith, Greg Giachelli, and Georgia Owen. Most people thought that CDF was the lucky and favored choice for new industry prospects, but the truth was that CDF developed a strategy involving several areas of expertise, and I will list only a few of these.

When computerized technology made its appearance, we had access to a list of national and international companies that sold their products between Augusta, Georgia, and Los Angeles, California. The growth of each compared to the place where the products sold were manufactured gave the CDF valuable information as to who would be a likely candidate to relocate to the Northeast Mississippi region. TVA helped CDF develop this list of prospects, and CDF was initially the exclusive possessor of this information. This information was of special interest since transportation costs are a major part of marketing a product. The railroads and truck lines also contributed to this information base. Among the two top costs for manufacturing are transportation costs and labor-management costs. CDF used strong research to extract information from the best labor information library in the state as recorded by the Mississippi Employment Security and the State Tax Commission, along with the US Database labor costs. The information was broken down by the CDF staff by SIC (Standard Industrialization to Classification), and it was custom made for each client-prospect in simple enough terms. A prospect, after having been asked to provide information about the proposed labor requirements of a new plant, would receive from the CDF staff a labor-cost budget figure when a site analysis was underway. The same was true for transportation when market destinations were furnished. In addition to this number, a local district and annual labor-rate analysis by each category of workers was given in detail as reported by the North Mississippi Industrial Association and Three Rivers Planning and Development District. As a special incentive, CDF kept a record of rates and fringe benefits of several area industries that could be used. The sources of such information were not revealed publicly, but they were used on a confidential marketing plan.

Usually, when the prospect visited with a site-seeking agenda, the prospect would want to visit two or three selected companies to talk to the human resources manager and/or the plant manager. With the advanced information that visiting prospects obtained, they were already knowledgeable about rates and fringe benefits, but this fact was not announced to the host of the visit. This strategy proved exceptionally important in the marketing process in that the visit was a validation of information supplied by CDF before the visit. This process also aided local industries and gave the existing industry managers reassurance that the new company was not going to get its rates excessive for that SIC number. This initiative was another one to add to the credibility of information supplied by CDF and the new location. Consistently, prospects were complimentary of the quality of the data and research along with the verbal and documentary presentation, which were among the highest quality they had encountered nationally.

The professional staff members were very knowledgeable of the feedback about CDF, and because of this recognition, they were collectively inspired as a team to do a better job in their respective division of responsibility and assigned performance areas. In fact, on several occasions, the staff was asked to do analyses on projects. Tupelo and Lee County were not competing with cities such as Corinth and Senatobia. Several projects in Itawamba, Prentiss, Pontotoc, and Tippah counties were analyzed, plus some out of state. The relationship with these clients made them feel obligated to give to CDF a future client as a project for CDF that they would have an influence upon in the future.

While we at CDF were making many available locations, most of our competition for prospects was continuing to use personal persuasion and usually pet projects of community leaders as marketing tools, when the real emphasis needed was on solid research based on the facts that help compute the probable profit the company would make at the new location. Most of our competition had their own agenda, which they used upon the arrival of the prospect, while we learned early that the only agenda we needed to use was the one that was developed by the prospect. From the beginning point at the hotels and airport, they wanted to see only the things that were on their list. We discovered early that prospects generally did not care to see the CDF office, the courthouse, or city hall, and they did not care to meet committees of public or business leaders. Their emphasis was on getting facts about sites, labor, productivity, availability of labor training facilities and help with transportation and storage facilities with rail access, highways, quantity, and quality of the utility service, and the cost of gas, electricity, water, sewer, projected need, availability of industrial and maintenance service, and local contractors. Most often we were reminded that the recreation, restaurants, quality of shopping, public services such as libraries, law enforcement, and residences were not overlooked; they were measured by literacy levels, crime rates, and living costs and had already been accessed before the visit.

We also learned early not to show our homes as an incentive. I once took a prospect to a home on a lake in northwest Tupelo where I was reminded that the prospect had a 15-acre lot on Lake Michigan, and he reminded me that what I was trying to show him was a house on a farm pond. On another occasion, Agnes and I tried to entertain a prospect at a local restaurant and learned that he had had dinner two nights prior in Paris, France. A Japanese client did not want to go to a golf course, but he made a special request to see Elvis's birthplace and the Elvis Presley Lake. The CDF marketing for industrial and commercial clients did offer alternative items for the visitor but always depended on the client to make the flexible schedule because most often high-level decision makers for the prospect would allow only one hour on the visit for fact verifying and validation of the information being received.

The general public and some community leaders never understood why CDF developed industrial sites like the Tupelo-Lee Industrial Park, South; Turner Industrial Park; Tupelo Industrial Center; the Adams Farm Site at Belden; Airpark Industrial Park; and the Harry A. Martin North Lee Complex. In fact, they were not located in dispersed geographic locations for several reasons. It is good to remember that to get businesses to build in a specific area, a desirable plant facility must meet the client's needs. One of the major reasons that the rural sites are always preferred is the client does not like double taxation from two local government entities, traffic congestion, or close-by residential areas. Rural sites are preferred, and our plan offered two or more sites in different locations, thereby giving CDF an edge. The second reason is that extending the job location to the edge of the population base offers an expanded labor market in multiple directions. All observations and research indicated that a job site generally extends 35 miles in each direction, and as an example, a 35-mile reach from Verona to Shannon would expand the local labor market to more than four times its normal size. This policy also allowed the local labor market to include primarily skill training from Itawamba Community College, but it also included other training facilities such as the Golden Triangle, Northeast Mississippi, and Northwest Alabama. Industry locators came to us at CDF with specific requirements, and most were not negotiable. We located a Chicago-based company that preferred workers who lived in a rural area rather than the urban area.

Another reason for the rural location of the industry site was that it allowed new large sites to enter the competitive market at competitive rates.

CDF had a policy to distribute the growth across the entire area so that more people would benefit. The primary manufacturing industries usually did not want to be in the back yards of others; instead, they wanted product suppliers they used to be in the vicinity. This plan allowed more to benefit from the value added, in terms of jobs and tax base, especially the schools; this philosophy was the basis for what Mr. True D. Morse proposed when his Tupelo Plan was presented in the late 1940s. Because the strength of Tupelo is in the region, growing the region must be the main goal of CDF. His economic growth and job growth plans were area-oriented and not city or county centered. For this reason, he advocated participation by mostly county leaders that did not follow political lines.

The Contributions of Kyle and Erin Brown

A couple that took a special interest in Agnes and me early in our stay in Tupelo was Kyle and Erin Barnes Brown. Kyle was a farmer, agricultural supply store owner, manufacturer supply agent, and his business thrived on Court Street as Brown McCully Farm Supply. Kyle pioneered in promoting pre-planting use of herbicides, in growing cotton, a major source of area farmers' cash crops in the 1940s and 1950s. Without any manufactured farm equipment for the application of the herbicide, we devised a contraption made of two large cotton gin pulleys, a tongue to pull it with, his Oliver tractor, and a power take-off from a small water pump and a ten-gallon tank to hold the mixture for spraying behind the pulleys as they rolled down the two rows. As crude as it was, it worked and was in high demand in a multi-county area. From this successful experiment, we two couples became acquainted and continued as good friends.

Erin was the secretary to V.S. "Josh" Whitesides at The People's Bank and Trust Company from the time of the reorganization of the bank after the Depression. He and his assistant, Mr. C.C. Eason, were a team that served from the 1930s to the time she retired, which was well into Mr. Eason's term as a successor to "Mr. Josh." Erin's family, the Barneses, were early settlers. She grew up in a pioneer home southeast of the GM&O Railroad on top of a hill where Barnes Crossing Road and the Old Saltillo Road intersect. The mall near there now is named Barnes Crossing Mall because there was a "doodlebug" stop to pick up GM&O Railroad passengers at this point that was named after the Barnes family. Most people today will not know what a railroad doodlebug is. It was a self-propelled railroad coach designed for very short runs; it was very inexpensive to ride. I recall that Erin said that she attended Tupelo schools as a girl and rode the doodlebug round trip to and from Barnes Crossing for a nickel a day.

Two members of the Barnes family served on the board of supervisors; one was a member of the board when the existing courthouse was built. Kyle led a movement to hard surface the roads in the county so rural residents would have a year-round way to get to the city for shopping, to market their farm produce, and to go to work off the farm. Rural off-the-farm workers and labor have been one of the strongest points in recruiting new industries and trade because usually, work ethics were better with these workers. Kyle also was a strong supporter of progressive ideas such as those being sponsored by CDF at the time.

It was in the early years of our careers in Tupelo that Agnes and I decided to get a second car. My work with the cooperative extension service required that I attend conferences, camps, training courses, and educational trips out of town, sometimes for a week at a time. We were living on a small budget, but we needed a second car so that Agnes could have a way to go while I was out of town. Kyle Brown led us to Mrs. Maude Carothers' home, located at that time off Clayton Avenue on land that Jim and Sue McCullough later owned. Mrs. Carothers lived in an attractive farmhouse with a front porch that was almost always occupied at that time with Mr. Charlie Carothers, in his favorite rocking chair. When we arrived, we were met by Mrs. Carothers and led to a one-car garage that had a car covered with a quilt and was obviously not used much. She uncovered the Model A Ford that had about 15,000 miles on it but was in excellent condition. It seemed to us that she considered the car to be a member of the family, and on the first visit, she would not say that she would sell it to us. We later learned that "Miss Maude" was Kyle's half-sister, and she needed assurance that the car would be treated well before she sold it to us for $400. Little did I know at the time that Agnes and I would later buy Mr. Charlie's relatives' birthplace at 1100 Clayton Avenue in Tupelo that was built in 1880 by his relative, Porter E. Carothers (1844-1923), and his wife, Mary Elizabeth Carothers (1854-1937).

Mr. Carothers was a Confederate veteran and an outstanding legislator, businessman, and large farmer. The Carotherses were on the board and were one of the organizers of the Peoples Bank (now Renasant) initially, and he also was the state legislator that introduced the legislation that established the State Highway Commission in the 1914-1916 period. This legislation is reported to have been in cooperation with U.S. Senator Bankhead's authorization of approving an automobile highway from Birmingham, Alabama, to Memphis, Tennessee, initially, and later from the United States east coast to the west coast. The highway was known as the Bankhead Highway; in Tupelo, it ran along Clayton Avenue and the Old Belden Road. A second route went through Pontotoc.

The Influence of Leo Zuber

It seems to me that Mr. Leo Zuber, one of the South's leading recognized planners, was influential in developing the plan that built the Downtown Mall and the person who approved Tupelo's application for the first in the state renewal grant. He supervised the planning for the redevelopment of downtown Atlanta, Georgia. Mr. Zuber was well ahead of those in leadership positions because he recognized, in the late 1960s, after a week of studying and visiting all the organized city and town leaders and visiting several of the rural open country neighborhoods, such as Birmingham Ridge, Brewer, Dorsey, Union Baptist, Union, and Unity, that each had very desirable people and physical characteristics, and all needed recognition for leadership that advanced the area.

He advocated for the formation of a formal organization of the Council of Governments; the formation of the council of towns and cities was the same idea advanced by Mr. Morse in the late 1940s because the council platform meant that these units would remain independent of rules and regulations except those offered by the state and federal government. Since all nine cities and towns that touch Lee County were originally agricultural towns and villages established along early routes of the Native American trails, the horse and buggy roads, the early railroads and most of the regional roads for autos followed the railroads and usually were close to or parallel to the nine population centers. All these settlements and urban areas had a different culture and background for selecting their leadership and growth and development policies. It was not until the Council of Governments was formed that any formal cooperative agreements emerged. We all have been aware that under a democratic free economic system that the more competition exists between units, the more growth occurs in the marketplace.

The council, or COG, has been and still is taking advantage of maximizing the stability and growth of all units, including the rural or open country territory that surrounds a larger region because doing so produces the resultant prosperity of the larger region. Usually, when a larger central city is established, there is a tendency for the state to take taxes and revenue from the large area, and when it is appropriated, the revenue return is restricted to the municipality and county boundaries. This outcome is especially depressing to area growth, and where the most of the cities' and towns' revenue comes to the units using tax, this revenue is restricted to the boundaries by politics and by law.

Because of visionary planning by the consultants – including True D. Morse, Leo Zuber, Dr. Bernard Weinstein, Dr. Harold Kaufman, and other specialists – the Tupelo Plan emphasized that the strength of the central city as a population group depends upon its ability to develop the entire region and not just the area within the city limits. During the past sixty-two years, a successful occupational structure had been established, and many components were well-established. These include the dispersion of the major job centers throughout the region and the establishment of a regional water system and its effective efforts to fully develop the regional, state, and federal highway system; additionally, the promotion of skills and higher educational opportunities came to the entire area. There is no other area in the state that has in place the structure and long-range visionary economic development planning as is present in Lee County and its influence in the Northeast Mississippi area.

Beware the "Pet Project" Syndrome

The "pet project" syndrome is always present in all community planning, and this area is not immune to this philosophy. This syndrome distracts or disorients the group's long-range efforts to advance this area. The generational change also affects long-range policies and strategies for growth. The individual grab bag for credit and recognition is most often destructive and a diversion from the real avenue for long- time progress. Attention to the personalities rather than attention to the principles, mission, and purposes is often the negative factor that stops progress. The longer we study the economic growth and development of this area of Northeast Mississippi, the more we realize that some of the most important leadership that caused major change and growth has been and still is in the transportation segment: railroads, highways, air, federal roads such as the Natchez Trace Parkway roadway, and local thoroughfares. Recently, there is the Tennessee-Tombigbee Waterway, which has much to contribute in the future.

Contributors to the Development of Northeast Mississippi

I wish to name a few of the leaders that I encountered in person or discovered through research and make a brief statement as follows. Among the first on highways was Porter Carothers, a Confederate veteran who lived west of what was then Tupelo on the Bankhead Highway, and he was the person credited with passage of the legislation that established the State Highway Act. Obviously, Mr. Carothers and Senator Bankhead of Sulligent, Alabama, served in the Civil War together and worked as a team to get the Bankhead Highway built to Tupelo and to Memphis from Birmingham. Mr. Carothers was also one of the founders of The Peoples Bank (now Renasant) that serves a five-state region.

The first highway commissioner was Mr. Will Robbins of Tupelo, who was a pioneer in building the first concrete highway in the South in 1916, which came into and out of Tupelo. A section of this historic road has been restored between Birmingham Ridge Road and the City of Saltillo. This road allowed the farmers to get in and out of Tupelo to market their products in difficult weather when roads normally became impassable in the prairie-type soils that are prevalent in this area. These soils are exceptionally good in producing livestock and crops, especially cotton. Cotton production and dairying were the backbones of the local economy, and these early transportation improvements such as the railroads and the highways enabled the area to grow and were where the people chose to build their homes and reside.

Another early leader was George Henry of Nettleton; he was president of the Frisco Railroad that came through Nettleton in 1888 because the city was a major source for hardwood timber.

According to the GM&O Historical Society's *Condensed History of the Railroad*, Colonel William C. Falkner, a Southern gentleman, lawyer, and statesman, in 1872 chartered the Ripley Railroad Company to connect his plantation interests in Ripley, Mississippi, with the Charleston Railroad (now Southern) at Middleton, Tennessee. The name was changed to the Ripley, Ship Island and Kentucky Railroad; later after the line extension through New Albany, Mississippi, to Pontotoc to the Gulf and to Chicago, the system became a part of the Gulf, Mobile and Northern Railroad. Colonel Falkner's association with early railroad development and promotion of the GM&O could be construed to be the basis of the GM&O's title as "The Rebel Route."

The person who deserves the credit for forming the GM&O, a railroad that continuously has been one of the driving forces behind the Tupelo and economic development of the region, was Mr. Isaac Burton Tigrett of Jackson, Tennessee. In 1940 the GM&N merged with the M&O, creating a system almost 2,000 miles connecting the ports of Mobile, St. Louis, and New Orleans. Thus, the Gulf, Mobile and Ohio Railroad was born. Because of the interest Mr. Tigrett had in Tupelo and the region, the resource of the railroad and the highly professional people who worked with him and the railroad, Tupelo leadership received his personal support and economic development advancement.

Several projects, which were highly supported and advocated by the GM&O Railroad, were a part of the growth and development of Tupelo. Among those things that I encountered in my career was the early work this railroad and the Frisco promoted in support of school children going to Jackson, Memphis, and other out-of-the-area events. The two railroads worked together through their passenger promotions of events to get the students special rates to travel to these destinations to further the adventure and education of the students. The two railroads and public relation agents promoted the special rates to encourage trips to the Mid-South Fair and to the state capital, the state Legislature, and other historical places and events. These promotions attracted hundreds of ordinary citizens, schoolteachers, and their students, which were in greater numbers per family at this time. The influence on the hundreds of students, teachers, civic leaders, and parents who brought information from other places certainly had a positive influence and added a sense of adventure and interest in the larger communities' willingness to seek positive change as part of building the area's culture that had broken down to the provincial attitude that resisted change. This positive step forward has been present and continues to be a valuable part of our heritage.

It was Mr. Tigrett's personal acquaintance with Mr. J.P. Nanney, mayor and president of The Bank of Tupelo at that time, that led to the acquisition of Day-Brite Lighting of St. Louis, a major company that has been in Tupelo since 1946 and was the first industry to employ principally men. At the time, the county had about 1,900 people working in industry, and most were "cut-and-sew" female employees. Mr. Tigrett also had a personal acquaintance with the Day-Brite leadership and was the person who influenced the company to come to Tupelo.

The next major area of industrialization in Tupelo came in 1948 when Rockwell chose Tupelo upon the recommendation of the Fantus Corporation of Chicago. Once again, Gulf Mobile and Ohio Railroad officials were extremely active in the preparation of the presentation and site selection information for the Rockwell plant. A request was made for the Rockwell plant to be served by the railroad; without Rockwell having to do any of the financing, the GM&O Land Company paid the cost, and the location of Rockwell was made possible. The Land Company acquired the railroad right-of-way for the construction of the track to the Rockwell property line. Later, the GM&O Land Company bought 21 acres south of the old Lee County Cooperative property all the way to the present Eason Boulevard and the GM&O main line where Malone & Hyde, Southern Pipe, and most of the *Daily Journal* buildings are located. The railroad company built a flood-control levee around all this property and later sold most of the remaining undeveloped land to the *Daily Journal*. The flood-control pumps and levees remained until after the Town Creek Flood Control Program was completed, and Dam 15 B was built west of the Natchez Trace Parkway and south of McCullough Boulevard.

Another example of help from the GM&O Land Company occurred when the Community Development Foundation expanded The Tupelo-Lee Industrial Park acreage, streets, and utilities east of the railroad's main line for these extended developments. Community Development Foundation did not have the ability to finance this extension through its credit sources. I worked out with the officials in Mobile, Alabama, a 10-year guarantee to pay the principal, interest, and balance off to the local banks during that period, or the GM&O would pay the note off and take possession of the assets. This transaction was extremely important to the future economic development in Lee County because this area was the preferred location for new plants. Because industries were attracted, and jobs became available, this area is still the largest employing industrial center in Lee County. The guaranteed "take-out" provision of the letter of credit was never used by the Community Development Foundation because revenue from the developing sites grew at a fast rate, and it later provided the basis for this industrial park to be nationally recognized for its growth during a challenging period of industry location.

There are many examples of how the railroads have been a major factor in the economic growth of Tupelo and Lee County, including allowing the city to acquire original railroad property, some of which was returned to private ownership. The value of the former railroad property in downtown Tupelo can be seen in the development of off-street parking that otherwise would not be available. Without the personal involvement and cooperation of GM&O and Frisco officials, this development would not have been possible. Officials set up several meetings for other officials and me to visit the Chicago and Springfield, Missouri, offices to work out details. The Tupelo Industrial Center at Veterans and Eason and the early Reed Industrial Park were served by the Burlington (Frisco) Railroad. National Springs, Rich Toys, B&B Concrete, and Tupelo Concrete Block Plant required Frisco Railroad participation in the early stages of the Community Development

Foundation's program to industrialize the area. Major industries such as Norbord at Guntown, Southern Diversified Industries at Baldwyn, E.R. Carpenter, Tecumseh, Sara Lee, and many others have had professional and monetary support from the railroads.

As I reflect on my 52-year career, of which more than 44 were spent with the Community Development Foundation, I hope to point out who, where, and how Tupelo obtained the information, technology, and vision building that led to a progressive program and leadership. There are dozens of officers, writers, and visitors who have become obsessed with what has been done here in economic and community development. Few, if any, ever ask how the details and base were built to assimilate all the factors and place them in a forward-moving vehicle that carried the daily burden and weight that must be borne for any substantial change in people's attitudes, values, and goals. It is my observation after looking at some of the most successful programs in the country, after visiting several European countries on recruiting ventures, and after having taught a national economic development leadership conference for a week in Australia, that few people care to understand the mechanics of a successful program – much less the essential parts that make it "run" or "function" productively. Most get motivated only by the adventure of the journey or the personal association with other travelers making the journey.

I am reminded of the character to whom I often refer. That character was James "Jim" Hoffman of Mansfield, Ohio, who made a necessary traveling stop at Walter Harrell's Gulf Station on Main Street in downtown Tupelo in the 1950s. I was reminded on February 16, 2010, after the city of Tupelo authorized a demolition company, Rayon Ford LLC of Saltillo, to demolish one of the most attractive and often photographed (in the 1950s) homes in Tupelo to be torn down and all debris removed. The lot was cleared for a new home construction in the future, and the house is being built now. At the time, it was anticipated that the house would be built alongside new upscale homes in the neighborhood where Federal Judge Claude Clayton once lived. In this area, one of the most talented and recognized commercial artists in the South-state area, Herbert Armstrong, also lived, as did two of Tupelo's most recognized industrial engineers, W.B. Fields and Charlie Rousseau, both of whom helped keep the cut-and-sew industry operating and productive. Sadly, a house was built and destroyed in a little over 60 years. The reason this house is mentioned here is that it was the home of the key volunteer community leader who worked to secure the Jim Hoffman plant and brought about several other significant economic events at that time.

Mr. J.M. Savery was chairman of the Draft Board of Tombigbee Electric Power Association (TVA's local distributor for two counties) and the Mississippi-Alabama Fair and Dairy Association. The combined Fair and Dairy show was an important event for the area's economy in the 1950s because agriculture was still the economic base of the region. Mr. Savery and Mr. Julius Berry, another insurance agency head, were also a competitive and very active part of the volunteer team that helped the Fantus Company bring Rockwell to Tupelo in 1948. Joining them were Mr. R.W. Reed, Sr., Mr. M.C. "Pat" Dougherty, Mr. J.P. Nanney and Mr. S. "Josh" Whitesides, along with multiple furniture store owner, Mr. Billy "Boss" McClure, Mr. George McLean, and several others. I never knew from where Mr. Savery got his leadership position, but I do know, and I observed very carefully that when there was a tough job ahead, he was a person who did the job. He was what I refer to as a "go-getter." I must include the furniture market originators: Lynn Davis, V.M. Cleveland, Dr. Ed Meek (Ole Miss), Ed Neelly (CDF Chairman), Harry Martin (CDF President), CDF staff and Jimmy Pappas (hotel owner). Other leaders were Joe Wiygul, Roy Black, and Bill Moran (FMC).

In reflection of thought, as I write these notes, I consider this to be the turning point in making the Community Development Foundation more effective. It was at this time that I started to put the staff and organization together through a very organized effort. The CDF expanded and brought a more powerful influence on the growth and development of the Tupelo-Lee County region. I will try to outline these changes in some detail in my future notes.

The CDF's Influence on Growth and Development

First, volunteer leadership is essential to community and economic development, but a fact must be recognized, and that is that there are three kinds of volunteer leaders: Those who are against progress, those who are on the "fence" and those who are for progress. The key is to have more than fifty percent in a democratic organization who favor positive change. Unfortunately, often an individual cannot be a very active agent for positive advancement and be loved and very popular. Accordingly, change-agent leaders are seldom elected in a democratic environment. After 52 years of professional experience as a participant (eight years with the extension service and 44 years with CDF) in one of the most successful rural development efforts in the Tupelo area of Northeast Mississippi, I note some observations regarding the structure and reasons for the excellent economic growth record.

Several groups of people/professionals were involved. I have named them as (1) The Architects, (2) The Visionaries, (3) The Professionals who served as group leaders, and (4) The Open-Minded Volunteers.

The Architects

(1a) Architects Associated with CDF:

RCDC
CDF
True D. Morse

(1b) Architects Not Associated with CDF:

J.B. Tigrett (GM&O)
Bill Beasley
Maurice Fulton (Fantus Corp.)
Bob Ady (Fantus Corp.)
T.T. Martin (V.P., GM&O)
Joe Christian (Frisco)
Mississippi Planning and Development
Randy Kelly (Director Three Rivers Planning District)

The Visionaries

(2a) Visionaries without Industrial Backgrounds:

M.M. Winkler, Sr.
George McLean
W.C. Dougherty
W.J. Pernell
Alice Little

(2b) Visionaries with Industrial Backgrounds:

Bill Dunlap
Kyle Brown
J.C. Whitehead
Mark Ledbetter
John A. "Red" Rasberry

The Professionals

(3a) Professionals without Industrial Backgrounds:

Sam Marshall
Truman Brooks
Harry A. Martin
Alice Little
Morris McGough

(3b) Professionals with Industrial Backgrounds:

Ralph Carnathan (TVA)
The staffs of the Agricultural and Industrial Department
Mississippi Planning and Development and various other consultants

The Open-Minded Volunteers

(4a) Open-Minded Individuals Associated with CDF:

Guy Mitchell, Sr.
J.P. Nanney
V.S. Whitesides
J.M. Savery
Gartrell Milam
Bob Reed
Bill McClure
Gordon Houston
P.K. Thomas
Paul McElroy
Herbert McCain
Area RCDC Council

(4b) Open-Minded Individuals Not Associated with CDF:

World War II veterans
Lee County Board of Supervisors
75% of the general public

(4c) Black Leaders and Other Community Leaders:

Tommy Lee Shack
Mrs. Claudy Bell
Al Gilmore
Hosie Holloman
Curtis Stovall
Rev. D. S. Rainey
Kenneth Mayfield
Tommy Ivey
Jake Flemming
Jimmy Lee Ivey
Richard Cleveland
Mrs. George Worthen
Frank Dowsing
Harry Grayson
Alice Little
Gay Benson

Joe Clark, Alice Little, "Red" Pernell, Harry A. Martin

Banks made low- to no- interest loans to buy 4-H Club calves.

The industrial development of Northeast Mississippi was led by the team of volunteers along with one of the most experienced professional staffs that received national and international recognition by major development agencies and publications on economic development. The group also received recognition from the federal government level by the Office of Budget and economic development agencies including the USDA Graduate School at Silver Springs, Maryland. The talents of the staff were diversified, and the combination made for a very strong team.

A major change in population in the South happened when people relocated to the industrial centers of the North; the trade area lost about 18,000 people before 1965 when the economy became more industrialized as a result of the actions of the True D. Morse CDF influence. Adjoining counties came together to make efforts to provide jobs, and as CDF called it, "better jobs with better pay." The CDF became an example of how a rural community can effect national economic growth with attention from several international countries.

The CDF was among the most effective groups that stabilized population movement in rural America by encouraging unusual growth in industrial jobs, which increased from less than 2,000 in Lee County in 1950 to more than 18,000 in 2000. These above-average quality jobs stimulated the opening in the health care and service sector of an increase of more than 30,000 jobs. This superb effort completely stabilized the out-migration to the point that, in the 1960s, Lee County began a period of major extended growth of population and jobs. This model of achievement was visited by and influenced many state officials and other state groups that used or tried to use the philosophy and technical methods in a large and extended number of political economic and community development organizations. The Tupelo Model Program was visited by representatives from more than 50 other countries. Records of many of these activities and events are recorded in the publication, "A Legacy of Excellence 1948-2000," by the Community Development Foundation. This publication is available at the Tupelo-Lee County Public Library.

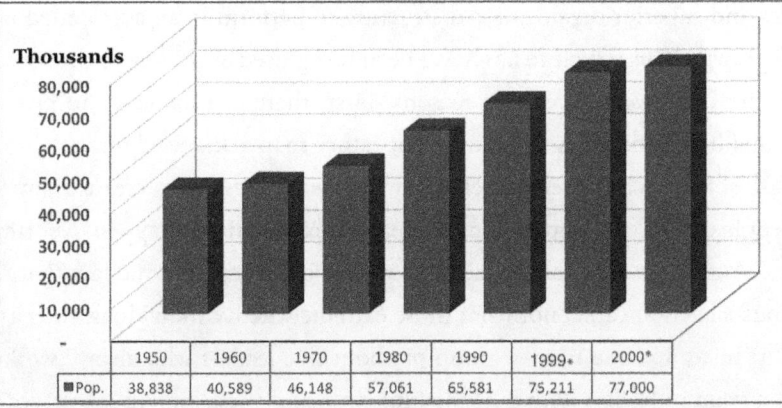

In the middle of the 1960s, the Mississippi Research and Development Center was established, and the two regions of North Mississippi projected to grow the most by Dr. Kenneth Wagner and his staff were the Greenville area and the Golden Triangle area that encompassed Columbus, Starkville, and West Point. The Tupelo area was not projected to be in the race for economic and population growth; however, history and the record of progress between the 1960s and the year 2000 point to the superior achievement of the Tupelo area and the surrounding counties. The leadership was determined to be at the forefront of growth in the state.

From the beginning, the CDF-led group had the technical characteristics and superior organizational structure to perform in an accelerated rate of growth. This structure has never been recognized as the key to the success of the CDF for at least two reasons. First, there is a tendency to give an individual credit for a single moment rather than acknowledging the broad base of leaders and their leadership, which was necessary to create a way for people to contribute to making something extraordinary happen over time.

Another reason for the lack of recognition arises from the fact that the unusual action came, not from those extremely active individuals such as I, but, instead, came from a group of about five leaders who always worked as a team of leaders with a defined mission, and these individuals served as a balance wheel for growth. The mission of the CDF was developed and implemented by the best architects, visionaries, professionals, and a group of open-minded citizens.

The reason I used the Jim Hoffman of Penn Tire as a real character in my narrative was that he actually tested and observed the stability of the CDF to stand firm when attacks came from the supporters of old no-growth, traditional, limited and closed-door approaches against those individuals who propounded new and advanced methods and fostered outside input of advanced and new ideas.

The people who challenged the idea of Penn Tire's coming to Tupelo had forgotten M.M. Winkler's recognizing the potential of True D. Morse's ideas on rural development and what those ideas could mean to the region around Tupelo. The challenges overlooked Mr. Winkler's broad interest as an accountant in the economic growth of the local area. He had convinced Mr. Morse and Mr. McLean to meet and discuss the long-range possibilities and results. Mr. Winkler's foresight helped to make possible a CDF that was ready to roll with a large base of public support at the time of Mr. Hoffman's visit to Tupelo. This support had been built mainly through more than 50 rural community development organizations in a five-county area. CDF also had the legacy of Sam Marshall and his successor, Truman D. Brooks, along with excellent development and management professionals to build the structure that preceded my term of service. Mr. Winkler also set up the CDF as a C 6 non-profit organization, which allowed it to operate on a regional basis.

It was at this stage that the area interest rose above the special interest of the urban power base in Tupelo that had been established through years of tradition. It was at this time that the leadership of the CDF and its management staff began to look at the area and regional needs as provided by its original charter of incorporation, which had been insisted upon by Mr. Morse. This process involved a multi-county mission and need rather than a single municipality mission and need. At this point, the architects of industry and manufacturing job growth convinced the visionaries that area employment must be considered a priority. The attitude of the employers referring to employees as "my employees" had to change. Employers had to accept the view that employees were individuals in a larger labor-employing market who were free to pursue better or different jobs if they so desired. This right is granted by law to the citizens of the United States of America. As such, they could move on without a later penalty or handicap by the former employer or his restricted employment confederates.

In most rural communities, the long-held traditional attitudes prevailed in the state and the region. Such attitudes and policies restricted newcomers from entering the labor market. The opening and extending of the opportunities for jobs gave the CDF a step up on its competition for Fortune 500-type employers. The most stabilizing group in the Tupelo area was made up of World War II veterans who saw that upon returning to their local neighborhoods and communities that they were restricted from or denied the employment they needed because existing industry leaders sometimes acted in such a fashion that they kept other jobs from being created in the area. Such actions often occurred because the leaders at that time were simply fearful that any new job opportunities might be in areas that would provide competition with their products or for job-seeking employees. Industry officials and company management who had done well and made a lot of money while the veterans had been serving their country were now in the way and were either controlling or interfering with the creation of new jobs within the areas where the veterans now lived.

CDF leaders broke the traditional practice by establishing absolute guidelines and policies on employee pirating and on avoiding the recruitment of employees if it would seriously damage the existing employer. These CDF-CRA policies strengthened once again the recruitment of new plants because the new company would have access to experienced workers to start the new plants, but it would have the protection of not being robbed of its employees by someone else in a new startup operation later. The CDF backed this policy, and it was a proven strong part of the recruiting strategy.

It is important to note that once again the change came from architects on the national scene and was not the product of a local person. The locals were visionaries and developed a very strong professional administration to make the initiative succeed. The formation of the CDF and the enactment of a nationally recognized job creation effort by CDF were two of the many efforts that have met success and gained much recognition at several levels of critique.

The idea was first presented to Dr. Harold Kaufman, representing the Social Service Center at Mississippi State University. Dr. Kaufman and his associates did extensive research on the CDF and organizations in other competitive rural areas. The group published several pamphlets and papers on the reasons for success. One of the most applauded CDF policies was the one that mandated the seeking of the architects in the country to help lay out the possibilities unseen by local leaders. Most reports and writings on Tupelo's success give credit to one or two people for progressive and consistent growth. This type of recognition helped to foster an incorrect perception that it was a one- or two horse-drawn movement. The reports did not recognize that the strength and success of the CDF and programs it selected were powered by a large, diverse group of leaders who were interested in the success of the project that had been selected. These multiple and diverse leadership groups were not motivated by just a few people, as was often reported.

Dr. Kaufman wrote, after extensive social science research sponsored by Mississippi State University and the National Mental Health Foundation and the participation of several senior professors of rural sociology, that what had been found was collaboration for performing small community development task forces on selected projects, all autonomous and independent of central control in all areas, except for budgetary overruns. This early approach stimulated the formation of many very active volunteer task forces in multiple areas of community and economic development.

Among these projects were the establishment of the first rural development councils, four-lane highways, regional water supply distribution centers, a coliseum, a farm and livestock arena, a farmer's market, and multiple industrial parks, which were strategically placed to enlarge the labor market population. In addition, there were projects in the performing arts area, such as the Gum Tree Festival, a symphony orchestra, and a visual arts center. Other projects included the establishment of the Council of Governments (the first in the state of Mississippi), the "Rally in the Valley" in support of the Tennessee Valley Authority, Industry-Education Day, which emphasized the teaching of economics, job training programs, and the building of the Advanced Education Center on the Tupelo campus of Itawamba Community College and the University of Mississippi. Other projects resulted in a community relation association, nationally affiliated neighborhood watch groups, and several economic symposiums. These are merely examples of programs initiated under the sharing of leadership responsibilities advocated by the CDF up to the year 2000 when I retired from the CDF.

The downside of this method of development is that one listens to many of the members' pet project ideas and to some suggestions from public officials who contribute little to the progress of the larger area. The operating policy established by the officers and the board of directors of the CDF led to a very innovative and productive community development and economic development period because it allowed the CDF to lead the accelerated growth of Northeast Mississippi, exceeding the state-selected future growth centers, namely Greenville and the Golden Triangle Area.

Almost always overlooked and seldom recognized were the prominent role and the large contributions made by the leadership of Mississippi State University, including the presidents, the sociology and extension service, and experiment stations personnel, and the district county and home agents. All these groups helped the RCDC and the CDF during the first eight years with untold hours and state-budgeted funds, which were used to promote many RCDC and CDF programs. Of special help was the power and influence of extension service officials, and especially, W.J. "Red" Pernell and such people as Mr. Dougherty and Mr. McLean regarding the acceptance of the True D. Morse Tupelo Plan.

The provincialism was so great between town and country people, among the different counties, it was the broad support of the district and state officials of the extension service who helped to change the strength of narrow-minded views. Mr. Pernell was an ex-officio member of CDF's board and executive committee during the first eight years and was the person who directed the organizational structure that Mr. Morse had recommended be implemented to expand the vision and mission of the "new" CDF.

As a student in 1947 from the School of Agriculture, I had been assigned by Dean E.B. Colmer to document and report on the new, emerging programs until my return to work with Mr. Pernell in 1948 as his assistant and later, as his associate. I was included in all the early meetings on policy formation as a note taker for Mr. Pernell. He was the balance wheel between Mr. Dougherty and Mr. McLean and kept the early programs on a progressive, but common-sense direction. Mr. Pernell was not only the key to the early organization's policy, but he also directed a nationally recognized Jersey Cattle Club, as well as a staff of outstanding extension service agents.

This staff was the only group in Mississippi to receive the Superior Service Award by the United States Department of Agriculture during this period.

From the beginning, the RCDC and the CDF recognized the importance of the excellent rural community leadership and especially the black influence on the growth of the area. There was no better representative in the program than Miss Alice I. Little, who, at that time, was designated as a Negro extension agent. The people who know the real facts about the early development of Tupelo and the Lee County area are aware of Miss Little's contributions and her community and church leadership. She was highly respected and became an important element in the Mississippi State University team that helped form the character of the RCDC and the CDF.

One factor that helped many of the black leaders in Northeast Mississippi was the fact that, unlike the rest of the state, many of the black families in Northeast Mississippi owned their own farms and were independent economically, even if some of the farms operated at the subsistence level. Lee County had very few members of the black population who worked at servant-only jobs. Mr. Harold Arrington, an African-American, became an influential county agent and has been very helpful in the further development of the African-American leadership of Lee County.

In 1947, the CDF, in cooperation with the Mississippi State University Experiment Station, established the Verona Branch of the Mississippi Experiment Station. The original land plot proved too small over time, and additional land was obtained adjacent to the property in the late 1950s. The MSU Experiment director and the CDF staff worked out a lease-purchase agreement between the University and the CDF that was accepted by the three locally-based banks in Tupelo. This action allowed for the needed expansion of the station in the late 1950s.

Another project on which MSU and the CDF worked together was the location of the Agriculture and Livestock Center sponsored by the Lee County Board of Supervisors. The center was built on the campus of the experiment station following the purchase of some additional land by Lee County. I hope that my narrative here will help document that CDF's record of growth and development involved the support and expertise of members of the MSU staff.

Mr. True D. Morse and his organization were recognized by the USDA agencies in the early 1940s as the foremost group of experts in the United States in the area of rural development. I wrote earlier that Mr. Morse was later appointed undersecretary of agriculture during the Eisenhower Administration; naturally, his area of responsibility involved rural development. As I have previously related, Dean E.B. Colmer of the MSU College of Agriculture wanted to know what was being planned in Tupelo in the summer of 1947. I was selected to spend six weeks working out of Mr. Pernell's county agent office, and I not only received semester hours credit, but I was also paid a salary to do a write-up of the proposed project. This opportunity led to the later adoption of the National Rural Development Program during the Eisenhower Administration. As you can see, the alliance between Mr. Morse, the USDA, and the state universities was important nationally, but most especially, in CDF's implementation of the Tupelo Plan.

The extensive studies done by the Social Science Center and the sociology department of MSU under the direction of Dr. Kaufman revealed avenues where successful development strategies could flourish as they had in Northeast Mississippi when multiple county participation existed.

"A LEGACY OF EXCELLENCE" REVISITED

In the statement I wrote for "A Legacy of Excellence," I summarized the key aspects that made CDF one of the top job development agencies of the nation because of the talents and execution efforts of the executive staff of CDF. This section of the report/memoir is devoted to the reflections of several former staff members who played a key role in the CDF and the COG.

NICK CHANDLER WROTE ON MAY 1, 2010:

"Dear Mr. Martin,

"The Tupelo story, in my opinion, can be summarized as the right people with the right gifts in the right place at the right time to make the Tupelo area a nationally and internationally recognized model for community and economic development.

"Solomon wisely said, 'Where there is no vision, the people perish.' I hope it's not too presumptuous to add where there is no organization and work, the people also perish.

"While much credit must be given to the vision provided and work done by countless community leaders, volunteers, staff members, and consultants over the years, without the extraordinary organizational and management skills of the enormously gifted Harry A. Martin, I believe that the Tupelo story would be a very quick read.

"I appreciate your asking me to contribute to your literary efforts, which I hope include a 'How To' textbook which addresses ongoing changes in community and economic development and offers potential strategies for the future.

"With 'Be innovative and creative' ringing in one ear and 'I want what I want and that's all I want' ringing in the other, I'll close and await a call from you regarding the efficacy of this epistle and the need, if any, for additional information."

Tom Bailey wrote on September 1, 2010:

"In the summer of 1974, I had just graduated from Tupelo High School and landed a summer job working for the Community Development Foundation. It was a tremendous opportunity for an 18-year-old who during the previous summers worked hauling cattle across the country and cleaning air conditioning units for Sears.

"The CDF'S mission was true to its name: It developed communities. It worked not just to recruit new jobs and expand existing businesses, it helped strengthen all areas that make a community healthy and appealing.

The organization didn't just build industrial parks: it worked to help improve the Tupelo area's educational systems, transportation networks, other infrastructure such as water and sewer lines and even the quality of local civic leadership.

"So, what on earth could a teenager do to contribute? Executive Director Harry Martin entrusted me with a specific project for the summer. Go out to the small, rural communities surrounding Tupelo, introduce myself to the residents, learn all I could about their communities, and identify their leaders, resources, and concerns. I was to take notes, write my observations, and report back to Mr. Martin by summer's end. He gave me a three-ring binder in which to put all the information I was to gather.

"Mr. Martin had called me into his office to give me this assignment. I can't recall the exact words, but I've always remembered the gist of something he stressed during our meeting: To complete the project, he said, to know all the community leaders, to truly learn the character of each community, to understand their hopes and challenges, and to fill the binder with this information, I'd have to stay focused, keep working, not get distracted, and finish the job.

"So, I spent the summer in small, unincorporated communities like Cedar Hill, Palmetto, Brewer, Auburn, Chesterville, Friendship, Evergreen, Union, Old Union, and Unity. These were communities long active in the Rural Community Development Council (RCDC). Each met monthly, and I would attend each meeting that summer, help support the leaders, and take group photos of meeting participants for the three-ring binder.

"I remember the active RCDC folks being warm and inviting. I've never forgotten the bib sack of homegrown tomatoes given me by Joe and Emma Estes of the Evergreen community. I remember being delighted to happen upon Mr. Dowsing of the Palmetto community, who was the father of Mississippi State football great, Frank Dowsing. And what a delightful surprise it was to knock on a door in the Cedar Hill community and have it answered by my first-grade teacher from Church Street Elementary, Mrs. Hinson.

"I also had the privilege that summer of working with Nick Chandler, who served the Lee County Council of Governments out of the CDF offices. Much of Nick's work that summer, as I recall, involved the highly detailed job of extending water and sewer lines to communities that have such infrastructure. I still have an impression of Nick's dogged patience and focus in nailing down the rights of way, parcel by parcel. Nick was a very slim young man with moppish blond hair, a gentle nature, and frequent smiles.

"I turned in that binder at summer's end, though I can't quite recall how full of information it was. I do remember completing my summer at CDF with a far greater understanding of the kind of detailed, community-building work that had made the organization such a success over the years."

On October 26, 2010, Gara Maleska wrote:

"I don't think the enclosed is what you had in mind when you asked me for a reminiscence of the CDF, so I will not be offended at all if you decide it has no place in your memoirs of the CDF. You specifically said you did not want to get into personalities, but the people I met in the CDF office... Margaret Nichols, Alice Little, Virginia Walker, Gloria (What Was Her Last Name?) to blustery Mr. Berry to gentlemanly Mr. McLean (who could still 'bring the hammer down') to congenial businessmen Bill Beasley and Bill Dunlap, to 'Cholly' (as I heard you call Mr. Holladay – I think I read years ago that he either earned a doctorate or received an honorary one, which is why I used the title in this article) who seemed too good-natured to be in such a demanding job...What good friends you had, Mr. Martin. And, how fortunate the CDF was to have them supporting it. Then, there was Mr. CDF himself – Harry Martin.

"I double-spaced my memory for ease of notations or corrections. After all these years, many 'facts' might not be accurate (perhaps LIFT does not stand for Lee-Itawamba-Fulton-Tupelo...?) and I have no facts at all such as what the first budget was. Fifty years have erased a lot from my memory... not reading the *Journal* daily has helped other facts recede or even be completely obliterated.

"I am sending this 'snail-mail' because as I told you on the phone, I don't use a computer or laptop and have managed ok so far, although my sons insist that I cannot continue to get by without one. I must admit that when I pulled out my Smith-Corona electric typewriter to type this (I thought I was set for life when I bought it in the late '70s) I realized how antiquated it is – and how heavy! I am not even sure I can find replacement ribbons. My son was showing me their new iPad when I was over there last week, and I admired it, of course, but don't want one myself. It will be obsolete by next week, and there will be another 'must have' at a higher price...

"I think your endeavor to write a history of the CDF is great and that it will be a tremendous gift to future generations of people in the area…"

Gara attached the following to her letter:

"The Community Development Foundation was founded as an organization to enhance the lives of the citizens of Northeast Mississippi, and it has fulfilled its purpose admirably through the years.

"In the mid-1960s, President Lyndon B. Johnson declared a War on Poverty, and the Office of Economic Opportunity was created. Many of the goals of the OEO were what the Community Development Foundation had already articulated and had been working on for years. Far-sighted leaders of the CDF realized that funds from OEO could be available to augment their own efforts. Thus, LIFT (Lee-Itawamba-Fulton-Tupelo), under the guidance and patronage of CDF, was established and later spun off as an independent entity.

"At that time, there was no public kindergarten in the area's schools, so the initial emphasis was on a program called Head Start. It was decided that every child – not only those at or below the poverty level – deserved a head start in education, therefore, the program was available to all pre-school children in the area.

"Head Start would emphasize the fundamentals (colors, shapes, numbers, letters, how to behave in a group, how to recognize and respond to the authority of a teacher or group leader, etc.) that should be mastered by and familiar to a child before entering a formal classroom.

"Consultants such as Dr. Charles Holladay, superintendent of the Tupelo City Schools, and Dr. Roscoe Boyer, professor in the College of Education at the University of Mississippi, contributed their enthusiasm and expertise in writing a proposal that was accepted and funded by the Office of Economic Opportunity.

"By 1969 the same philosophy of early education which the CDF had emphasized in its grant application for a Head Start Program for Northeast Mississippi was utilized and incorporated into a show on PBS which has had generations of viewers and myriad emulating shows for children on TV: the beloved *SESAME STREET*.

"As LIFT became incorporated and autonomous, some of the early programs initiated by CDF mutated or became extinct, but the one I remember most vividly and fondly almost fifty years later was Head Start."

Reflection

As I walked the rounds in the Mall at Barnes Crossing in Tupelo on an early December morning in 2011, memories crossed my mind. While recalling my 63 years of living as an adult, I thought about the families who farmed the land involved with the development of the mall campus. I remembered the Ruff family and its large herd of Holstein cattle, cotton acreage, and acres of silage, hay, and grain grown for feed for the livestock. I remembered the sound of the first mechanical equipment – the "putt-putt" of the two-cylinder John Deere and the motor on the Oliver tractor owned by a neighbor, Kyle Brown. These two tractors were among the first farm machines that were replacing the mules, steers, and horses that the early settlers used in the earlier days of the settlers' cultivation and, in some cases, used in the woods for logging purposes. The McCulloughs and the Kings, along with the Greens, all owned property where the mall campus now exists. The Bristows were to the south, and the Cochrans were to the west. Kyle Brown was married to Erin Barnes, whose family settled east of the M&O Railroad tracks. The extended family owns land in the Oak Hill, Mooreville, and Skyline communities. As I reflected, I remembered that these families were connected to early settlers all over the area even before Lee County was formed in 1866.

The nice concrete and clay tile floor I was walking on in the mall was located where crops and livestock were grown after the Tupelo gum tree and other natural timber were removed so that the very rich, alluvial soil could be made to contribute to not only the economic well-being of the families but also to the benefit of the community at large through financing, production of products purchased, taxes, and income from products grown, which at the time was the most creative of the growth techniques known and the most impacting source of economic growth in rural America.

A transition was made from the basic constructive use to one that is part of the most major stimulus to the retail market: a major regional shopping area with an estimated annual attendance of over 12 million people, envisioned by Mr. David Hocker and Associates of Kentucky. In real estate and economic development circles, the mall is known as a business generator that helps stimulate more economic growth, and because shopping is now considered to be the top entertainment event of the American people, the mall venues must have something interesting and exciting for all ages. The Mall at Barnes Crossing has these features and, as a result, is one of the highest sales-producing malls per square foot occupying dollar volume among its competitors in the region. The twelve to thirteen million visitors provide evidence of its economic generator power.

The payroll base of industry workers gradually grew and formed the financial support for a quality medical environment of several hundred skilled health care professionals – an expanded employer base that joined the industry base for solid economic growth.

As the CDF president representing the Board of Directors with expertise, and technology developed by Dr. Bernard Weinstein, I am very proud to have been instrumental in assisting with the acquisition of Dr. Weinstein's services and the study that determined that a regional mall was an economically feasible project; however, as with True D. Morse's original writing of the Tupelo Plan that called for multi-county leadership and participation, the traditional and self-appointed leaders resisted any changes in the direction of community development efforts. There were the "old money" Tupelo leaders who tried to ditch the project since Tupelo already had two malls, even though those malls were outdated. This group argued that we ought to force through an aggressive program of persuasion that there should be absolute loyalty to existing businesses rather than the free market principle of capitalism that is almost always successful. At that time, there was the strong influence of World War II veterans on the board of the

CDF who had fought for individual freedom that supported the effort to open the area to a freer personal choice environment. This individual freedom should allow people to shop wherever and for whatever they chose to without direction from others.

The board approved the regional open-door policy for retailing and service businesses, and several potential developers were contracted, including David Hocker and Associates, who moved in and took the task of developing what Mr. Weinstein predicted could happen. In addition to the belief that individuals should choose where to spend their money, Dr. Weinstein pointed out to the group that the regional mall did not have to be in Tupelo but could be successful anywhere in the area that had the proper support facilities and automobile access.

As I reminisce on my experiences in building the most successful job creation agency in rural America between 1950 and 2000, represented by Lee County, I realize it is a small county in size when compared with the average county in Mississippi. I realize evidence proves that encouraging and assisting professionally the leaders of the counties surrounding Lee County with the largest growth in new jobs in manufacturing (see charts) of any comparable rural area in the country, has been profitable. Nevertheless, with the situation today as it was in 1947 when I made my study for MSU of Mr. Morse's plan, I realize that there is much unrealized growth and development potential yet to be captured. The big problem is the same today as it was then, in that traditional leaders want to fence in the project boundaries to their own territory that they control. During my administration, I saw manufacturing employment go from fewer than 4,000 employees to reach almost 19,000 in Lee County alone, by the year 2000. The manufacturing and the agricultural workers are the primary creators of wealth in the community with approximately 1.7 new workers added in service and trade for each of the above.

As I look back on the statement by General, and later, President Eisenhower that the "weak and timid do not protect the survival of freedom," they do not protect the important segment of being a free people, including independent living, with a strong ability to produce the sustenance needed for one's own family without the dependence on others to create the motivation or the "want to" to do what is necessary to prepare a person physically, mentally, or spiritually to accept the challenge to move oneself forward.

There has been success in the city and the county. This success has also created an element that thinks that someone else did all the work. It has enabled the masses to advance, so it is not necessary for individuals to express their own talents and natural abilities to advance those characteristics that are required to build a solid community, in which the area to live and raise a family is a desirable place. The decline in the quality of schools, fair and strict law enforcement, and freedom by so much of a part of the majority of Lee County's adult population from government-imposed regulations as a burden to homeowners are all perceived to be overdone rather than citizen-based on moral law and spiritual values.

As I look backward to the late 1940s, I recall that places like Corinth, Columbus, and Greenville were the growth places in North Mississippi and how Tupelo/Lee County was not looked at as an area of future opportunity. Through the adoption of Mr. Morse's plan to regionalize the economy of the area and being a part of that work team that was made up primarily of World War II veterans and their families, I recognized that community action groups can bring about positive change. I am also aware that from research and experience, I learned that there had been no county or city in the history of Mississippi that had been able to maintain an ongoing period of people and economic growth without shooting themselves in the foot. The charter of the Community Development Foundation in 1945 as an independent regional economic organization was the vehicle that carried the leadership and action for future growth.

With a family background of my ancestors living in the vicinity of Meridian and Laurel as settlers before the state was chartered, a family legacy of being a descendant of pioneer families in that area since about 1800, I heard stories about the growth of both Meridian and Laurel. Both reached a certain point in growth and became unsuccessful in sustaining their status. Since no place in Mississippi was ever able to achieve continued success, why would we here expect to achieve something that others in our great state could not achieve and successfully sustain? The symptoms of failure began long ago when Tupelo announced that it would not send its fire trucks to fight a county fire. They continued when the local leaders started to criticize area people for not shopping downtown in Tupelo. They continued when there were towns from Baldwyn to Shannon and Nettleton to Sherman with close long-established businesses and services, not to mention the loyalty of Fulton, Amory, Aberdeen, Okolona, Pontotoc, New Albany, and Booneville to help the leadership of the economic development effort from the late 1940s to the year 2000.

The selection of the Fairpark District for the city's major promotion and development project came at a time when its schools, law enforcement, area relations, and older neighborhoods were deteriorating reflected poor judgment from leaders. Streets and curbs needed upkeep and limited code enforcement and beautification at this time. Most of the available money was spent on reaching out and annexing some geographic areas of other government entities that had used good common sense and had become more attractive to a large number of new homes. A large number of these families were descendants of the older families of the area and had family and cultural roots in those areas of public policy rather than in the great cooperative spirit demonstrated earlier in Tupelo by Mayor James Ballard when he provided water and sewer and other services beyond the city limits without annexing the areas involved.

In more recent months, another of the many decisions from the city includes addressing the churches needing support about expanding the zoning for parking for churches that are facing a challenging situation about the use of family vehicles, especially if young people are involved in the family church attendance. With the greatly expanded population, churches must sometimes handle three vehicles for some family units in need of many more parking spaces to promote and sustain church attendance.

In the early days of Tupelo's history, it was known as a beautiful city, and also as a "church-going place." Church attendance nationwide is declining. If there are high school- and college-age people in a family, there are situations where each parent has a vehicle and the youth also, so there are considerably more vehicles per family that need parking space at church. In addition, we are living in an age when grandchildren and, sometimes, adult children are coming back home to live. This situation includes an increased demand for church parking. For some, the problem of not having adequate parking is seen as not a zoning issue but a moral and spiritual issue, and it seems that the church leaders are restricting the attendance and expansion of the church, which is sometimes referred to as "God's House."

Can We Know?[1] was the title of T.T. Martin's book he sent me with warm regards. It was a simple message about Jesus Christ furnishing a way to find ultimate completion as children of God.

The new approach to making a poor community become economically better and more progressive in economic independence at least comparable to a majority of other people in other states is more difficult than *Can We Know?* I have always found in my career that there are constantly present in most decision-making groups those individuals who have ideas and "special projects" that are not as important as the economic overall growth needed to lift the economic level of more people.

The words in the title *Can We Know?* are applicable to the leadership of CDF because it takes multiple people to make a major policy or new program work if it was the right direction to bring some development and economic benefit to the group that would lift the standard of living higher or raise the per-capita income reported. CDF worked with Prentiss, Alcorn, Pontotoc, Union, Itawamba, and other places to grow its economic base. I am proud of my opportunity to participate. Yes, the efforts received regional, national, and international attention.

Could we know if there could have been a better balance or even more appropriations toward keeping Tupelo's neighborhoods and the downtown

---

1 Thomas Todd Martin, Can We Know? (Mobile: Mobile College Press, 1986).

areas maintained? Can we know if the Lee County Agricultural Center could have been a partner of the Coliseum and been successful with some cooperation between the two policy groups? After all, agriculture was, up to 1960, the major income for the county and could not be removed. Can we know about their plans? Even though we put cash into the location of a large industry to help locate it in Fulton and worked with Travis Staub in locating a furniture industry in Fulton and assisted Buster Davis, a businessman in getting the waterway developed and funded, not all plans were particularly successful with the CDF and Itawamba County Development Association. The deal to make the port a two-county sponsored project was decided by a local group to keep Lee County from locating industry at the port. This outcome proves that special and political interests sometime impede economic growth. Even though there were a few failures, the very large and successful effort to lead in CDF bringing more wealth into the community in industry, trade, and technical education has not been achieved by any other county as to the rate it was in Northeast Mississippi. It was reported to the public in 2018 that the Southern Baptist Church's total membership had dropped by 192,000 from 14.8 million members. This statistic clearly shows that, as the largest religious group in Lee County, Southern Baptists are not immune to the declining church membership. The question remains whether we can do something at this time to increase church attendance. Furthermore, can we continue to see progress in our area?

Earlier I quoted President Eisenhower as saying that the "weak and timid" cannot move a project forward. It takes the band of leaders who have the ability to move things forward, such as several of the leaders of CDF between 1950-2000 who were World War II or other military veterans. To move Mississippi out of the bottom of family income of the 50 states, major changes must be found to improve the low level to a higher level. Can that be because in the past no area in our state has been able to continue its substantial growth?

T.T. Martin was right in his book; if we practice new and innovative projects and methods, we can know that the level of living and economic standards increase is a real goal for a region that can be achieved so it "can be done. For example, the new Fairpark District, located in downtown Tupelo, was planned and built to enhance downtown Tupelo and is currently being further developed as new projects are being considered. It is an impressive new economic development that other potential regional communities should consider emulating.

Harry Martin
CDF President (1956-2000)
Worked at CDF (June 1, 1947 – August 21, 2000)

Appendix I: A Listing of Accomplishments of Harry A. Martin

Harry A. Martin was the executive president and secretary of the Community Development Foundation, an 1,100-member, non-profit organization charged with the economic enhancement of the Tupelo/Lee County, Mississippi, area. As executive president, he was responsible for the growth and development of seven affiliated programs, including the Rural Community Development Council. Martin also served as the executive director of Lee County Council of Governments, a non-profit organization composed of local and state elected officials.

Martin was selected as the executive officer of the CDF in May 1956. Before his association with CDF, Martin served with Lee County Cooperative Extension Service as a leader of 4-H programs. While serving in this capacity, the staff was awarded the Superior Service Award by the U.S. Department of Agriculture. Martin also served as the associate Lee County agent in charge of farm and home planning, which was the first position and first program of its kind in Mississippi.

During Martin's 44 years of CDF service, he received numerous citations for his exceptional achievements in economic development and community organization. He assisted in more than 100 plant locations and expansions, and development of five industrial parks, leading to CDF's citation as one of the top 10 development agencies in the nation by *Site Selection Handbook* and the Industrial Development Research Council in Atlanta, Georgia.

The National Business Alliance and the U.S. Department of Housing and Urban Development selected CDF's service area, Lee County, as being one of the ten best examples of a public/private partnership in the country. This was recently re-emphasized with Tupelo's selection by the Ford Foundation as one of the nation's finest examples of public/private partnerships.

Under Martin's direction, the CDF built numerous large-budget public and private projects that have received great population-based support. He was the administrator of the Better Community Corporation and two additional non-profit housing organizations that maintain 92 units for housing physically handicapped, elderly, or low-income people. This project is designed to assist families in rural areas where such housing is generally not available.

One of Martin's main contributions to the Community Development Foundation's success was his ability to focus on "hands-on" projects. By bringing all segments of the community into a project, he utilized diverse skills and talents available within the region and "community ownership" of projects and programs. In this manner, he assisted in such diverse programs as developing a regional water supply system, establishing a national model for technical career development program for high school and junior college students, and attracting the location of IBM's Principles of the Alphabet Literacy Laboratory at Itawamba Community College's Tupelo Campus.

Model programs coordinated by Martin attracted large national and international audiences to the region. International graduate students in Vanderbilt University's economic development program have traveled to Tupelo/Lee County annually to study the innovative Rural Community Development Council communities. Through this program, Martin created the infrastructure for off-farm employment of rural people, while preserving the integrity of the small farm by offering markets for products grown by part-time and full-time farmers. The RCDC program has served as a model in rural economic development since the 1950s and continues to be a thriving resource for the region.

As a long-time supporter of the Tennessee Valley Authority, Martin organized the 1985 Regional Rally in the Valley. The Rally, attended by more than 500 people, demonstrated public support for TVA programs and served as a model for later rallies held throughout the TVA service area.

In 1989, Martin served as a keynote speaker at the Rural Revitalization of Western Australia Seminar at the Muresk Institute of Agriculture, Curtin University of Technology, Northam, Australia. Many of the technological programs and projects that have been successful in Northeast Mississippi have now been adopted for Western Australia use, and in 1990 Martin received an invitation to Australia to serve as a consultant and later was named the Outstanding International Community Developer.

In September 1989, Martin was a member of Governor Ray Mabus' European Economic Tour.

A native of Quitman, Mississippi, Martin served in the U.S. Air Force during World War II. He is a graduate of Mississippi State University, where he earned his bachelor of science degree in agricultural administration, and, as a Horace A. Moses Federation National Scholar, he completed advanced organizational courses at Colorado State University.

In 1958, Martin served as the district governor for Civitan International and in 1959 was named Tupelo's Outstanding Young Man of the Year. In 2000 he was named Man of the Year in Lee County by the Civitans.

Martin has served on numerous state and national advisory committees, including the advisory committee for Undersecretary of Agriculture True D. Morse, and the Eisenhower task force to develop a national rural development initiative; the Tennessee Valley Authority Council; and Mississippi's Constitutional Convention Commission.

He was a member of the executive committee of AHEAD (Advocating Highways for Economic Advancement and Development). In 1987, Martin coordinated AHEAD's Highway Day, a state rally that attracted more than 1,000 supporters for a comprehensive four-lane highway program for Mississippi. Subsequently Mississippi legislators passed a $1.6 billion highway bill to fund four-lane construction for 1,077 miles of highway over a 14-year period.

He was a charter member and secretary/treasurer of the Tupelo Furniture Marketing Association, a non-profit organization charged with development and marketing furniture made in Mississippi, as well as promoting the Tupelo Mississippi National Furniture Market, a semi-annual furniture exhibition in Tupelo.

Martin was president of the Mississippi Association of Chamber of Commerce Executives for the 1989-1990 program years.

He was a member of the board of directors of the Mid-South Common Market, a regional development association based in Memphis, Tennessee.

He was a member of the board of directors of CREATE, which chartered a community foundation that administers sizeable grant funds for projects and activities in North Mississippi.

He was secretary/treasurer of the tri-state Natchez Trace Parkway Association, and that group was the leader in securing funds from congress to finish the roadway.

He is a past president of the Mississippi Christian Community Fellowship in Starkville, Mississippi, and of the Southeastern Community Development Association, which was the first such organization formed in the nation.

Martin and his late wife, Agnes, have one daughter, Janet, and he resides in Tupelo, Mississippi.

Appendix II: A Historical Life Sketch of Harry A. Martin

- Attended Hebron Ridge School beginning at the age of 4.

- Attended Cedar Creek School for one year.

- Attended Hopewell School through grade 8.

- Graduated from Quitman High School in 1942.

- Attended Mississippi State University, 1942-1943.

- Enlisted in the Air Force, October 1943-1945.

- Attended Air Force cadet training.

- Inducted at Camp Shelby, Hattiesburg, Mississippi.

- Underwent testing and basic military training, Miami Beach, Florida.

- Completed basic air training, Lockbourne Air Force Base, Columbus, Ohio.

- Underwent academic training for the Air Force, University of Pittsburg, Pittsburg, Pennsylvania.

- Completed preflight training, Freeman Field, Seymore, Indiana.

- Attended the San Antonio Air Cadet Training Center, San Antonio, Texas.

- Attended navigation school at Ellington Field, Monroe, Louisiana.

- Finished navigation school, discharged late 1945.

- Graduated from Mississippi State University in 1948.

- Received BS degree in agricultural administration.

- Worked in Dean E.B. Colmer's office keeping records on part-time farm and grading papers while a student.

- Was a member of KME Honorary Mathematics Fraternity and usual agricultural clubs.

- Accepted teaching position upon graduation in June 1948 at Clarkdale High School (on Clarke-Lauderdale County Line) for the summer of 1948. Resigned October 1, 1948, to take a position with Lee County Extension Service as assistant county agent in charge of Boys 4-H work in Lee County.

- Excelled in preparing dairy herds for shows, winning all championships in 1949 in state except Junior Championship at Newton, Mississippi, show. Initiated "Cow Purchase Plan" with three banks cooperating so hundreds of boys and girls could own their own dairy animals.

- Had several state-winning 4-H teams. Received the Horace A. Moses Scholarship and attended Colorado State University to study advanced organizational work.

- Was a member of the staff of the Lee County Extension Service when it received the "Superior Service Award" from the USDA.

- Was appointed associate Lee County agent to do balanced farming and home planning for the first position and first program of its kind in Mississippi and was patterned after the Missouri Plan.

- Elected as secretary-manager of the CDF in May 1956. Elected as executive director of the Lee County Council of Governments in 1970. Served as director and secretary of CREATE, Inc.

- Served as president, lieutenant governor, and governor of Tupelo Civitan Club and Mississippi District of Civitan International. Received the District Honor Key on two occasions and was named Outstanding Lieutenant Governor of the Mississippi District of Civitans. Chartered 29 new clubs while governor.

- Served as president of the Southeastern Community Development Association in 1961. This group pioneered the Community Development movement in America, with Tupelo, Mississippi, and Ashville, North Carolina, as leaders.

- Served as president and secretary of the Mississippi Christian Community Fellowship, a statewide non-denominational organization.

- Served on the advisory committee for True D. Morse, undersecretary of agriculture, when the National Rural Development Program was formulated during the Eisenhower Administration.

- Served as co-chairman of Regional Veterans Information and Service Conference in Northeast Mississippi.

- Served as chairman of the committee that developed the organizational structure for HOPE, Highways Our Pressing Emergencies, prior to passage of the $600 million-dollar Highway Corridor Program.

- Served as secretary of Better Community Corporation, a non-profit housing group in Lee County.

- Served as the first secretary of the Northeast Mississippi Economic Development Association.

- Served as secretary-treasurer of the area HOPE Fund raising organization.

- Developed the planning grant and served as first director of the Lift Community Action Agency of ORO. Was the founder and chief promoter of the Big Ten organization in Northeast Mississippi.

- Served on the state task force that wrote the state plan for State Vocational Rehabilitation Program.

- Served on the Appalachian Regional Commission Advisory Committee for job training and was appointed by Governor Finch.

- Served as disaster chairman of the Lee County Chapter of the American Red Cross for more than 10 years.

- Served on the board as County Fund Chairman for the Lee County Cancer Society.

- Assisted Julius G. Berry and Agnes Martin in formulating the organization of Lee United Neighbors, a project assigned to CDF to initiate.

- Was on a three-man task force that developed the organizational structure for the Northeast Mississippi Community Relations Association in 1959.

- Served as secretary of Lee County Better Government Group when major law enforcement reform was implemented in the 1950s.

- Serves on the M.C. "Pat" Dougherty Scholarship Committee.

- Served as secretary-treasurer of Lee United Companions, a group fighting illegitimacy among black females.

- Was named Tupelo's Outstanding Young Man of the Year in 1958.

- Received the Conservation Award from the District Wildlife Federation for promoting the reforestation of Lee County.

- Served as chairman of the Tupelo Centennial Commission in 1970.

- Served as co-chairman of the Tupelo-Lee County Bicentennial Commission in 1976.

- Served as coordinator of the High Flight and Christian Family Life Week Emphasis in 1976 and 1977.

- Served as chairman of the Mayor Prayer Breakfast for the years 1975-1977.

- As a youth, served as president of 4-H Club, served as president of FFA Chapter and the team that won district award in parliamentary procedure, won State Forestry Award, was second in state in health contest. Won Thomas Wilson Livestock Award, numerous top prizes in county and district livestock shows, and served as president of Clarke County 4-H Council.

- Played forward on the first basketball team of Quitman High School. Played on Air Force team of Pittsburg.

- Member of Calvary Baptist Church. Taught Sunday school for 20 years; deacon, 20 years, and served as chairman of the building committee and finance committee when the new sanctuary of East Heights Baptist Church was built.

- Served as a member of the Lee County Baptist Brotherhood Association.

- Served as a member of Pioneer Mission Team that went to western Colorado to do mission work for the Southern Baptist Convention.

- Conducted Lay Revival in Baptist churches in Nucla and Naturita, Colorado. Served on various committees of Lee County Baptist and Mississippi Baptist Association.

- Served as district fund chairman for the Greater Blue Mountain College Fund Campaign.

- Served for several years as secretary of Lee County Chapter of Mississippi State Alumni Association.

- Served on the board of Lee United Neighbors for 14 years. Was a charter member and co-chairman of the Museum and Historical Committee of the East Mississippi Historical Committee Northeast Mississippi Historical Association.

- Was a charter member of Christian Men's Association and served on the Board of Directors.

- Was a master Mason, Tupelo; Royal Arch Mason, Meridian.

- Served as secretary of Mississippi Polled Hereford Association for several years.

- Was a member of Southern Community Development Association.

- Was a member of Mississippi Association of Chamber of Commerce Executives.

- Was a member of Southern Industrial Development Council.

- Owned timber land since the age of 14. Interested in reforestation and management of timber land. Used proceeds of 4-H livestock projects to pay for first two years of college education.

- Partnered with brother in two Western Auto Stores in Quitman and Stonewall, Mississippi.

- Served as president of TV Cable of Quitman and Waynesboro, Mississippi.

- In 1958 appointed Honorary Chief of the Chickasaw Nation by Governor Maytubby. Commissioned as a Kentucky Colonel in 1983 by Governor John Y. Brown, Jr.

- Was a partner in WEMR properties of Saltillo.

- Was a partner in Beasley-Martin Real Estate in Tupelo.

- Was president of Associated Developers, Incorporated, Tupelo.

- Was the person who laid out and developed Lake Piomingo and Indian Hills.

- Enjoys reading, hiking in woods, gardening, collecting antiques, and traveling.

Appendix III: Biographical Sketch of Agnes Louease Norris Martin

- Born: November 27, 1924

- Clarke County, Quitman, Mississippi 39355.

- Parents: Elvin and Susie Norris (both deceased)

- One brother, Leon Norris (deceased)

- Married, Harry Martin July 30, 1948. (Her childhood sweetheart)

- One daughter, Janet Maria Martin

- Moved to Tupelo, Mississippi, October 1948.

- Served as a clerk in Agriculture Conservation and Stabilization Organization, Lee County.

- Served as the organizing office secretary of Lee County Neighbors (1963-1964).

- Was a member of Pilot Club

- Taught 25 years in Children's Sunday school at Calvary Baptist Church.

- Had a special interest in wildlife and forest preservation.

- Recognized for the entertainment in her home of industrial prospects and business, political, and industrial executives locating or moving to the Tupelo area.

- Served as a Girl Scout leader.

- Served as chairperson of the decoration committee of the CDF annual meeting and special occasion events.

- Mrs. Martin was also known for her skill in baking pound cakes for special occasions and for friends, neighbors, and nonprofit organizations.

www.ingramcontent.com/pod-product-compliance
Lightning Source LLC
LaVergne TN
LVHW041334080426
835512LV00006B/457